THE
COMMONWEALTH
IN ASIA

THE
COMMONWEALTH
IN ASIA

BY

SIR IVOR JENNINGS, K.C.

VICE-CHANCELLOR, UNIVERSITY OF CEYLON

BEING

THE WAYNFLETE LECTURES

DELIVERED IN THE COLLEGE OF
ST. MARY MAGDALEN, OXFORD

1949

OXFORD
AT THE CLARENDON PRESS

Oxford University Press, Amen House, London E.C.4

GLASGOW NEW YORK TORONTO MELBOURNE WELLINGTON
BOMBAY CALCUTTA MADRAS CAPE TOWN

Geoffrey Cumberlege, Publisher to the University

FIRST EDITION 1951
REPRINTED LITHOGRAPHICALLY IN GREAT BRITAIN
AT THE UNIVERSITY PRESS, OXFORD, 1952
BY CHARLES BATEY, PRINTER TO THE UNIVERSITY
FROM SHEETS OF THE FIRST EDITION

PREFACE

THIS book is based on the Waynflete Lectures delivered at Magdalen College, Oxford, in Hilary Term 1949. Publication has been delayed in order to use the final text of the Indian Constitution instead of the draft of 1948 upon which my lecture was based. I had hoped to be able to add a chapter on Pakistan, but so far only the text of the preamble is available. Chapter VIII has been rewritten in the light of the discussions which preceded the Conference of Prime Ministers in London in April 1949, and the Conference of Foreign Ministers in Colombo in January 1950. It is a coincidence, due to the date of publication of the Indian Constitution, that on the day on which the revised text of the book was completed and this Preface written, the Commonwealth—or at least the Foreign Ministers thereof—really was in Asia.

I am much indebted to the President and Fellows of Magdalen College for the hospitality which they accorded to me during my term of office as Waynflete Lecturer. It is impossible for those who teach in universities in England to realize how much we, who are attached to universities overseas, value opportunities for renewing our acquaintance with English scholarship. The debt is the greater when, as in my case, the visitor is an administrator whose main concern has been with building plans and government grants and the hosts a house so ancient and so distinguished as Magdalen College.

I have also to thank Mr. V. V. Giri, High Commissioner for India in Ceylon, and Mr. Salim Khan, Trade Commissioner for Pakistan in Ceylon, for placing documents at my disposal.

W. I. J.

UNIVERSITY OF CEYLON
COLOMBO
9 *January* 1950

CONTENTS

INTRODUCTION

ON 15 August 1947 India and Pakistan became Dominions with interim Constitutions formed by modifying the Government of India Act, 1935. The Constituent Assembly for India has completed its work, and a new Constitution making India a 'sovereign democratic republic' came into operation on 26 January 1950. The Constituent Assembly for Pakistan is still engaged in preparing its task and not even a draft has yet been published. On 4 February 1948 Ceylon acquired 'fully responsible status within the Commonwealth'—a synonym for Dominion Status—with a permanent Constitution formed by modification of its Constitution of 1946, which was drafted with this development in mind. All three countries have had the common experience of jumping straight from a status subordinate to the United Kingdom in most external affairs and in some internal affairs into a status of equality and independence within the Commonwealth. The older Dominions, on the other hand, were colonies with responsible government long before the status formerly known as Dominion Status was evolved, and the process of emancipation was slow.

Even more significant are other differences. The three countries are the heirs of a great and ancient tradition, or more accurately of several layers of tradition, with variations not only in each of the three countries but also in the several parts of each. The tradition did not include the ideas of democracy and nationalism, which are of Western origin and therefore recent additions to the social scene. Accordingly the elements of diversity, which may be classified as deriving from race, language, caste, religion, class, and education, are of greater importance than in western countries. All of them, except caste, exist in those western countries, but nationalism and democracy have there grown up in spite of them and have, wherever they have been successful, adapted themselves to the conditions which they have created. India, Pakistan, and Ceylon thus have a set of common problems which, though not different in nature from those of the West, are different in emphasis and importance and will have to be resolved if democratic government is to be successfully established.

The purpose of these lectures is to examine the problems thus created and to consider the tentative solutions which have been adopted or suggested. There is some advantage in viewing the position from Ceylon, not only because that island was the first to establish a permanent Constitution but also because the problems are less acute. The dividing lines, sharp in India and Pakistan, have become blurred partly by centuries of comparative isolation and partly by 450 years of western infiltration. Kipling's famous adage never was true of India; it is obviously false in Ceylon, where East and West have met for centuries and have produced a way of life which is neither exclusively oriental nor exclusively occidental. The task of the Ceylonese is therefore easier than those of the Indians and the Pakistanis, and they may possibly show the way towards a solution of the problems of all three countries.

The division of the old political unit called 'India' into the Dominions of India and Pakistan has created a problem of nomenclature. Though India, Pakistan, and Ceylon are in many respects different, they share a way of life and a culture which are differentiated from those of all other countries. It is not enough to call it Asiatic or, to use the term now preferred, Asian, because Chinese civilization has a different texture and the Muslim countries of western Asia yet another. It is not the tradition of the Hindu religion. It cannot be called Indo-Aryan, for Dravidian influences are strong both in India and Ceylon, and Islamic influences can hardly be regarded as Aryan. It seems convenient, therefore, to use the term 'Indian' to describe at times the characteristics which relate only to the Union of India and at other times to describe the characteristics which apply to all three countries. The Ceylonese will not object, for, though proud of their own achievements, they are also proud of their relationship with Mother India. The characteristics of Pakistan will no doubt diverge in time, but for the present the history which the Pakistanis share with the Indians is so important that they will perhaps not object to the generic term.

I

A DIVERSITY OF PEOPLES

THE sub-continent of India with its attendant island of Ceylon forms one of the most obvious geographical units of the world. Though invaders have poured in over the North-West Frontier and by sea, it has been sufficiently segregated to form a distinct physical type and a separate civilization. Great though the differences among its peoples are, there are yet common characteristics in sufficient number to justify the customary though politically inaccurate description of 'India'. It is true that it has never been a political unit, even during the short period of British rule; but Asia as a whole shows that political factors are not the sole determinants of social change. Though Ceylon has been politically distinct for centuries, its social context may still be described not inaccurately as Indian. In the long panorama of Indian history, which stretches for at least five thousand years, a few centuries are relatively unimportant.

The unity of Indian culture derives from the same sources as its diversity. Its origin cannot be traced. It seems probable, however, that the primitive tribes which inhabit the hills and the remote jungles are the relics if not of the aboriginal inhabitants at least of the earliest known inhabitants. The oldest surviving civilization is that associated with the four Dravidian languages of the south—Tamil, Telegu, Malayalam, and Kannada. It is possible that the civilization which flourished in the Indus valley at least 5,000 years ago was in its essence Dravidian. There are still Dravidian relics in north India. Moreover, all the Indo-Aryan languages, including Sanskrit, contain Dravidian elements; and it is significant that these elements relate mainly to the ordinary incidents of a settled agricultural life.

It is thus reasonable to infer that the primitive peoples now represented by the hill tribes once occupied the whole sub-continent as well as Ceylon, where the now almost extinct Veddahs did not differ fundamentally from the tribes of the continent. Dravidian civilization infiltrated over the North-West Frontier and spread over the easily cultivated portions of the whole area. No doubt the thickness of the layer varied from place to place. In the hills and the remoter jungles (including, perhaps, most of Ceylon) the Dravidian influence was weak. In the fertile valleys it was strong. The process was repeated perhaps three thousand or four thousand years ago, when Indo-Aryan influence began to infiltrate by the same route. As before, the thickness of the layer varied from place to place. In the south, for instance, the Dravidian languages were retained, though they came under strong Aryan influences. Elsewhere the Aryan languages prevailed but with the incorporation of strong Dravidian elements.

More significant than the diversity of language was the similarity of religion, for Hinduism is not merely a religion but also a type of social organism. If it were only a religion it might have spread through the Brahmans. It is, however, significant that the joint family and the caste system are to be found in all parts of India and Ceylon except in the north-west, where later invaders have virtually swept Hinduism away. Since neither is to be found in the earlier books of the Rigveda, the earliest Sanskrit text, it seems clear that Hinduism was either a Dravidian idea absorbed or developed by the Aryans, or a product of the fusion of Aryan and Dravidian ideas.

The wars and civil wars of the Hindu monarchies, which divided India politically, tended towards its fusion socially. When armies marched and countermarched, carrying off men as prisoners and women as booty, the racial composition of the population inevitably became more and more mixed. Emphasis is laid on 'race' in all three countries. Millions of people consider that they belong to one 'race' or another.

Endogamy is now strictly practised not only within the 'race' but also within the caste, and this gives the theory plausibility. Historically and ethnologically, however, it is clear that there are no 'races' in the biological sense either in India or in the West. To use the term 'blood' is scientifically misleading, but if it may be used as a metaphor it must be asserted that all the races of India are of mixed blood. There are differences of language and other social traditions which create differences of social inheritance. There are differences of colour, size, and physiognomy which tend to be perpetuated by the endogamy generally practised by the castes. There are differences of costume which emphasize and, indeed, exaggerate such social and physical differences as exist and help to enable an observer to classify the 'races'. As soon as an attempt is made to put physical differences on a scientific basis, however, the classification breaks down. Scientifically speaking there are no races; each of the so-called races is a group of mixed biological inheritance sharing a common social inheritance. The traditions of the race are handed down from generation to generation and endogamy hinders a fusion of cultures. The differences are social differences emphasized by physical differences, but a Tamil may look like a Bengali and a Sinhalese like a Gujarati. Biologically speaking, race is a fiction; culturally, it is a reality.

The distinction between the Aryans and the Dravidians is not a racial distinction. It would not be drawn if scholars, mostly European, had not interested themselves in the etymologies of the Indian languages. The fact that the Dravidian languages have persisted in the south suggests that on the Malabar and Coromandel coasts the mixture is more Dravidian than Aryan. The persistence of the dark skins and snub noses to which the Rigveda made somewhat contemptuous allusion—for colour prejudice is no European innovation —leads to the same conclusion: but there is no essential difference between the Hinduism of the south and the north, and ethnologists find it impossible to produce a physical characteristic which is typically Dravidian. The four Dravidian areas have nothing in common that they do not share with the other sections of India and Ceylon. 'Dravidistan' is an invention of modern politicians.

ISLAMIC INDIA

The Muslim infiltration which began soon after the death of the Prophet in A.D. 632 seems to have been of the same nature as the earlier Dravidian and Aryan infiltrations. The Muslims were of diverse ethnological origin. The Arabs, who were then the world's greatest navigators, came by sea, but they were not sufficiently numerous to make Arabic one of the languages of India. The Turks, the Afghans, and the Mongols entered by the North-West Frontier. Already of mixed 'blood', they intermarried with the Hindus and added further diversity to the Indian stock. As with the Dravidians and the Aryans the extent of the infiltration varied. In the North-West Frontier Province, Baluchistan, and Sind it was considerable. Elsewhere it was comparatively small.

The Muslims of the Indian sub-continent are not a race or a collection of races but the followers of a religion. It is, too, a religion of a type fundamentally different from Hinduism and its derivatives. Hinduism is indigenous and peculiar to India. Buddhism in its Mahayana form has spread to Tibet, China, and Japan, and in its Theravada form to Burma and Siam, but Hinduism can be spread only by exporting Hindus. It is not a proselytizing religion and it has not only its roots but its being in Hindustan. Islam, on the other hand, is one of the great international religions which unites Muslims as brothers in Islam across political frontiers, and in spite of wide diversities of economic status and biological origin. Islam spread in India not so much by the infiltration of Muslims as by the conversion of Hindus. Consequently, religion in India is no test of 'race'. Indeed, the change of religion often involved no great change of social convention. Even caste, which is theoretically inconsistent with Islam, has persisted among many Indian Muslims. The brotherhood of Islam necessarily minimized its effects. There are and can be no Muslim untouchables and the prohibition against inter-dining weakened where it did not disappear. Caste, in other words, merely created endogamous groups engaged in different occupations, as among the Buddhists of Ceylon.

The fact that Islam was external to India, had its centre in far-off Arabia, and had its authoritative texts in a language which was not spoken in India, made a fusion of cultures difficult. The court language of the Mughul Empire was Persian; but this in itself would not have mattered, for it could gradually have been relegated to the position of a classical language like Sanskrit. The vernacular of the Muslims of the Punjab and Hyderabad was Urdu, a variety of Hindi using Arabic script and incorporating Persian words. The evolution of a common language would have been no more difficult than, say, the fusion of Anglo-Saxon and Norman-French into English. In Bengal the Muslims, who were mostly converts, spoke Bengali. Had the firm and en-lightened policy of Akbar (1556–1605) been followed, it is possible not only that European infiltration would have been prevented in India (though it would have occurred in Ceylon) but also that a single culture, essentially Indian in texture, would have covered the whole sub-continent. His successors were not of his quality; the growing unity of India disinte-grated into anarchy which converted the Europeans from armed traders into governing authorities; and Indian unity was achieved, for a century only, under British rule.

THE EUROPEAN INFILTRATION

The Europeans, like the Arabs, came to India as traders, though the Portuguese were Christian missionaries also. The traders were compelled to arm themselves not only because of the anarchy consequent on the breaking up of the Mughul Empire, but also to protect themselves from each other. The distinction between trade and piracy and between piracy and

war was so fine as often to be unrecognizable. Having armed
forces and finding that even the dregs of English society sent
out from Europe could, with discipline, defeat the ill-disci-
plined armies of the Indian nawabs, they became nawabs
themselves. Nor was the process hindered by the fact that the
new nawabs (or nabobs) became as wealthy as the old, and
by the same methods—loot, bribery, tribute, and monopolies.
Ceylon, as usual, suffered far less than India. There the
Portuguese began to exercise powers of government in the
Maritime Provinces early in the sixteenth century. In 1646
they were superseded by the Dutch East Indian Company,
who were ousted by the British East India Company in
1796. The period of company rule was, however, short, and
in 1802 the island had the good fortune to come directly
under the Crown. By this time the worst characteristics
of 'Old Corruption' were being mitigated in Britain. The
Evangelical Movement and Methodism created new standards—or restored old standards—of morality. Benthamite
Radicalism emphasized the welfare of the governed. The
Colebrooke Reports of 1832 had all the defects of dogmatic
Benthamism, but they did emphasize that the government of
the people should be for the benefit of the people. Not every
action of the Government after 1833 can be defended, but
on the whole the island was reasonably well governed until,
quietly, peacefully, and efficiently, power was surrendered to
the Ceylonese in 1948.

The number of Europeans in India and Ceylon was always
proportionately small. The number of European women
was even smaller. Neither colour prejudice nor morals prevented the Portuguese and the French from marrying Indian
and Sinhalese women, with or without the blessing of the
Church. The English and the Dutch factors were stern
Puritans who frowned on what they described as immorality,
but the English in the East shared in the deterioration of
morals which followed the Restoration. Nor were they un-
affected by the tradition that women were lawful booty of

war. What is more, the European soldiers in the East were drawn not from the sternly moral Nonconformist middle classes but from the dregs of the English towns. The result was the growth of a substantial Eurasian population.

Where the caste system was rigid it was impossible for these Eurasians to be incorporated into Hindu society, and they tended to become a distinct caste. Even in Ceylon, where the caste system was much less rigid, the 'Portuguese Burghers' (as they were incongruously called after the British occupation) have only recently fallen back into ordinary Sinhalese society. The Dutch Burghers, whether of pure European blood or not, have retained their separate existence like the Anglo-Indians. On the other hand, the Sinhalese and even the Tamils of Ceylon do not lose caste by marrying European or Eurasian women: and though the practice being frowned upon is rare, the coming of the Europeans has in some measure added a further mixture to peoples who were already very mixed, in spite of caste endogamy.

The Europeans also brought Christianity. There was already a small Christian community on the Malabar coast, but under European influence it has become the second largest minority—second to the Muslims—in India and proportionately even stronger in Ceylon. Leaving aside its inherent attraction, there were four reasons for conversion to Christianity. The first was that under Portuguese rule it was virtually forced by the authority of the Inquisition. The second was that even under the British (at least until 1858) Christians were favoured in selection for employment. The third was that Christianity, like Islam, deprecated caste and was thus specially attractive to the untouchables and the lower castes. The fourth was simply the convenience of conformity: if one lived in a European settlement, where all the 'best people' were Christians and where other religions were regarded as idolatry and superstition, it was obviously more comfortable to conform. These influences were so strong in

Ceylon that at the end of the nineteenth century the Christians were optimistic enough to hope for the disappearance of Buddhism.[1]

The Christian deprecation of caste did not, however, succeed in abolishing it, even in Ceylon. In India the children of untouchables have generally to be segregated and interdining in school refectories is not always possible. Even in Ceylon there are sometimes separate churches for different castes. Both in India and in Ceylon intermarriage between Christians of different castes is rare, though more common than among Hindus and Buddhists.

Nevertheless, the European infiltration has resulted in fundamental social changes. For centuries the village economy remained fundamentally unchanged. The villagers grew their own food, spun their own clothes, built their own houses, and made their own utensils. Tribute, taxation, and rent (terms which are almost synonymous) were paid in kind. The rajahs and nawabs accumulated treasure and employed large numbers of retainers and craftsmen, but commerce developed first under Moorish and subsequently under European initiative. The great towns began to grow under British control, and it is significant that the largest of them, Calcutta, Bombay, and Madras, are still to be found in the earliest British settlements. In the towns the caste system, though persistent, necessarily became weaker in its incidents. Servants had to live together even if their functions were allocated on a basis of caste. Traders had to serve persons of all castes. Factories drew people of all races and castes into proximity. Roads and railways broke down provincial isolation.

The greatest change of all was the introduction of English education. Though theoretically available to everybody, it was in practice available only to those who could pay for it. Inevitably the great mass of the untouchables and lower castes were excluded by lack of means as well as social prejudice, but where available it cut across caste and communal

---

[1] See Bishop Copleston, *Buddhism*,

barriers. A person of sufficient initiative or good fortune who could by trade, money-lending, the acquisition of land, or otherwise earn enough income to send his eldest son to school could raise the status of the family even though he could not change its caste. The eldest son obtained government or mercantile employment and helped to educate not only his sons but his brothers and nephews also. They in turn obtained salaried employment or entered the professions, especially law and medicine. A class system was thus superimposed on the caste system, often resulting in the spectacle, strange to oriental eyes, of men of lower caste giving orders to men of higher castes.

This is especially noticeable in Ceylon, where English education was first introduced and has covered some 6 per cent. of the population.[1] The English-educated changed both language and costume. The 'trouser-karen' cannot be described as belonging to a distinct caste, because anybody can become a 'trouser-karen' if he can obtain an English education; nor did English education abolish the caste distinctions, because a Goigama (cultivator) will not marry a Karawa (fisher) or a Salagama (cinnamon-peeler) or vice versa; nevertheless, a 'trouser-karen' will not marry a village maiden of the same caste because, though he will not be outcaste, he will be de-classed. What is more, the Karawa and Salagama of the coast, having at once more initiative and greater opportunities than the Goigama of the interior, have in many cases obtained positions of economic dominance. The Kandyans as a whole consider themselves a depressed community. In following the tradition of 'blaming the British' they are historically more accurate than they are aware; for though there is no evidence that they would be less depressed if the Kandyan Convention of 1815 had not brought the Kandyan Provinces under British rule, and equally no evidence that they would be richer were it not for the tea and rubber estates, it is certainly true that the comparative wealth of

[1] About 11 per cent. of the literate section of the population.

many of the low-country Sinhalese is due to the introduction of western commerce, English education, and the estate system.

In India the effects are not so noticeable because the Brahmans and other caste Hindus took readily to English education. Among Hindus, therefore, the class system of the West has not caused such a considerable variation of the normal effects of the caste system of the East. Nevertheless, its political consequences have been fundamental. The English-educated class were for the first time given a common language, English. They also acquired a mature political philosophy having no relation to the traditional learning of India, but which was able to incorporate the ancient culture of their country. The nationalist movement was, and still is, an essentially urban, English-educated movement. It is true that it obtained mass support through the power and influence of Mahatma Gandhi and the appeal by the Muslim League to all brothers in Islam; but all the leaders have been and are English-educated. This is equally true of Ceylon, in spite of the adult franchise which has now been in operation for nearly twenty years.

It is significant, too, that the Muslims took to English education less easily than the Hindus, the Sikhs, and the Buddhists. English education spread mainly through Christian effort; and Muslims looked askance at the 'religious environment' on which Christian missionaries lay such emphasis. Many of the Muslims of India were either poor cultivators to whom English education was not available because of its cost, or armed retainers of Muslim princes whose services were no longer needed, except in the Indian Army, when British rule expanded. The Muslim boy's primary responsibility was to learn the Qurân in Arabic, and this required an effort which deprived him for some years of the opportunity of English education. Finally, purdah was stronger among the Muslims than among the Hindus, the education of girls beyond the age of puberty was virtually impossible until purdah schools were established, and this in turn gave the Muslim boy a less valuable home education than was available to the Hindu. In large measure, as we shall see, the communal problem of India was due not so much to the numerical predominance of the Hindus as to their wider adoption of English education. Under the Mughuls the Muslims were the governing class. In independent India, before Pakistan was created, the Hindus threatened or promised to become the governing class.

UNITY AND DIVERSITY

The peoples of the three countries are normally divided according to four methods of classification—race, language, religion, and class. Caste is a subdivision of race, for there are separate castes among the several races or language groups. Nor are the methods of classification either clear or mutually exclusive.

The classification according to race is obviously fictitious, for all the races are very mixed. Nevertheless, the term has to be used because there are distinct cultural groups to which political propaganda can attribute a common ancestry, and their case can be made plausible by the endogamy which is everywhere practised. In the main, the race is a language group, for language is the principal social inheritance, the resultant of the process of admixture by which the several layers have been created. Difficulties of classification arise where the language seems to conflict with biological inheritance. Thus on the west and east coasts of Ceylon there are groups with Sinhalese names whose home language is Tamil. Biologically, no doubt, they derive more from Aryan than from Dravidian ancestors,[1] though obviously they are of very mixed descent and they speak Tamil because it has been for centuries the dominant language of the area. If the Tamils were the larger community in Ceylon these groups would no doubt claim to be Tamils; the Sinhalese being the majority

[1] i.e. Aryan-speaking and Dravidian-speaking.

they claim to be Sinhalese. Since the one claim is ethnologically as good as the other, either is plausible because both are false.

Another difference between the racial and language classification is noticeable in Ceylon and perhaps in parts of India (e.g. Bombay) also. The westernized Ceylonese have adopted English as their home language. They know enough Sinhalese or Tamil to speak to servants, but among themselves they speak English and can neither read nor write Sinhalese or Tamil. Under the impulse of nationalism, however, this tradition is changing, and the new generation of parents is doing its best to speak Sinhalese or Tamil to the children. Legislation is giving stronger effect to this tendency, for since 1946 education in the first five standards has been through the 'mother tongue' defined racially. That is, the children of a person who claims to be Sinhalese are taught through Sinhalese even if their home language is English. The absurdity of this arrangement is, of course, minimized by the fact that the children who speak English to their parents speak Sinhalese (or Tamil) to ayahs and other servants. Further, students who claim to be either Sinhalese or Tamil are required to offer Sinhalese or Tamil at the Senior School Certificate, the Higher School Certificate, and the Civil Service Examinations. So far, however, these measures have not affected the social convention. It is bad manners to speak in Sinhalese—or even in Tamil—to a person who speaks English. The English-educated minority is the economically favoured class and for all practical purposes the governing class. To be able to speak English fluently is a sign of social prestige: to assume that a person can speak only his 'mother tongue' is to suggest that he belongs to the 'lower orders'. Nationalist politicians pass motions in favour of the national languages which their constituents speak, but they also ask for more 'English' schools because their constituents want to learn English to obtain the social and economic advantages which that language confers.

What is more, the coming of independence has created a breach in the solid front for the 'mother tongue'. If there were one local language the case for it would have been strengthened by independence: but there are two such languages—or, if the Burghers be included, three of them. How is it possible to develop a patriotic tradition and avoid communalism if the children are taught through different languages, in different classes, and adults of different communities cannot understand each other? There must be a common language: but if it is not English it must be Sinhalese: and for the minorities English is neutral, whereas Sinhalese confers an advantage on the majority. It has been urged that both Sinhalese and Tamil should be taught; but this will not solve the problem because English will still be required. The Sinhalese will learn to speak English and to pass an examination in Tamil; but the Tamils will have to learn to speak both Sinhalese and English if they are to compete on equal terms.

Indian opinion is suffering much the same evolution. The political reaction from English has been stronger because the struggle for independence was fiercer: but it is not easy to find a national language to replace it. Hindi is spoken over a wide area in the north, but the Bengalis, the Marathis, the Gujaratis, and the Dravidian-speaking peoples of the south feel that it would give an advantage to the Hindi-speaking peoples. On the other hand, English has not been the ordinary speaking language even of educated Indians, except among groups where there has been no other common tongue.

Whether race is defined according to biological inheritance or according to the social inheritance of language and other conventions makes little difference, for the groups are in any case endogamous. Even in Ceylon marriages between Sinhalese and Tamils are rare, rarer in fact than marriages between Sinhalese or Tamils on the one hand and Burghers or Europeans on the other. Where such marriages do occur the fiction of the purity of the race is maintained by the convention, rarely precisely formulated, that the children take the race or 'mother tongue' (defined racially) of the father. Thus the children of a Sinhalese father are deemed to be Sinhalese even if the mother be European, Eurasian, or Tamil. The only exception to this rule arises where the father is European. If the mother be Eurasian or Sinhalese or Tamil the European community does not regard the children as Europeans and accordingly they are classified as Eurasian, Burgher, or Anglo-Indian. Intermarriages between Indian and Ceylonese men and European women generally occur in the United Kingdom, where colour prejudice is weak, whereas intermarriages between European men and Indian or Ceylonese women usually occur in India or Ceylon, where prejudice is stronger. Consequently, the former are much more numerous than the latter. The rule is thus of much wider application than the exception; that is to say, the children generally remain in the races or language groups instead of swelling the number of the Eurasians. It is, of course, true that the number of people who are biologically Eurasian, because they have at least one European ancestor, must be very large. If a Portuguese father in 1530 had a Eurasian daughter who married a Sinhalese, if there were two children in each generation, and if there were no intermarriage among collaterals, the Portuguese ancestor would now have over 2 billion descendants. This figure alone shows that the assumptions are false, but it also shows how widespread may be the biological consequences of intermarriage. It is probable that the great majority of the people of the sea-coasts of India and Ceylon are biologically Eurasian. The rule that children take the race or language group of their father (unless he is European) enables the fiction of race to be maintained.

The origin of caste is a matter of dispute. It seems probable, however, that it is derived from three sources. First, it is a consequence of conquest, the conquered peoples being enslaved or treated as inferior beings. Secondly, it is a consequence of the obloquy attached to those callings which were deemed to be inferior or menial, especially those involving the taking of life (except in warfare) or association with human excrement. Thirdly, it arose from the enhancement by the Brahmans of their own power and prestige. It is argued plausibly that it was a factor which integrated social life. Each person occupied the status and followed the calling which it had pleased God to attribute to him. If his conduct merited it he might hope for a higher status at his next reincarnation. A highly complex and well-integrated social organization was thus created which met the needs of a static community. It was in fact a rigid class system in an age when rigidity was not undesirable. In the more backward villages it continues to fill this purpose, though it can hardly be defended on that ground according to modern western thought. With the growth of a new economic organization after the European infiltration and the development of steam and electricity, however, it became quite outmoded. At its best it produces endogamous groups which are irrelevant to modern conditions. At its worst it obstructs development through the prohibition of inter-dining and the persistence of untouchability.

Strangely enough the division which has had the most serious consequences in the political field, that based on religion, is socially the least important. In India it cannot be alleged that the Muslims are a distinct race, for most of them are descended from converted Hindus and in any case the Muslims have never been so strictly endogamous as the Hindus. In Ceylon the Muslims classify themselves as Moors and Malays, but this is obviously a complete fiction. The Malay regiments from whom the Malays are descended contained no Malay women and the proportion of Malay 'blood' in the community must now be very small. The Moorish community no doubt took its origin from Arab traders, but it is unlikely that they brought women with them. Also the language of the Moors is usually Tamil even in the Sinhalese areas, a fact which suggests that most of their ancestors came from south India. In the main, therefore, the Moors must be of mixed Sinhalese and Tamil descent with some relics of Arab ancestry.

Hinduism and Buddhism are tolerant religions which find it easy not only to allow their followers to live at peace with others but even to admit new and varied groups. Islam, like Christianity, finds it less easy to tolerate unbelief, and yet the Hindus and the Muslims were able to live in the same villages and to attend the same festivals. The conflicts which have arisen must therefore be due not to religion but to politics, using that word to cover the changes in political status which have occurred since the break-up of the Mughul Empire. The Muslims of India were once the governing class; they now regard themselves as a backward community. Sikhism, too, is not in itself a disintegrating force. Indeed, it developed as an attempt to integrate Hinduism and Islam. Christianity has not spread among the Muslims and the Sikhs, and among the Hindus and the Buddhists it has tended to create new groups of the same nature as castes. On the other hand, it has not produced a rigid endogamy, so that intermarriage among Christians and non-Christians of the same caste is not uncommon. It has thus helped to multiply the groups, but in the main its effects have not been disintegrating.

Class is the last of the disintegrating factors and is of considerable importance, especially in Ceylon, where it is evidenced by change of costume and change of language. The English-speaking 'trouser-karen' are intellectually segregated from the villagers and even from the workers of the towns. Where nationalism inspires repudiation of the European trousers, the segregation remains, for the so-called 'national costume', which looks like an English night-shirt, is as much a badge of class as trousers. The effect of class is heightened by the ostentation which requires the comparatively wealthy to ride in gaudy cars and to wear expensive sarees and jewellery. In India the class divergence is much less obvious because the local vernacular is generally spoken even by the English-educated and because under the inspiration of Mahatma Gandhi differences of costume are comparatively rare.

Class divergence is, however, greater even than the insignia would indicate. The extremes are the villagers scraping an inadequate living from a small patch of ground and the great capitalists of Bombay and Calcutta. The Europeans are no longer at the extreme; they are generally employees of limited companies enjoying a higher standard of luxury than they would enjoy in Europe, but no longer living like 'nabobs'. Ceylon, too, has neither extreme, for there the villagers are generally rather wealthier than in India and there are few capitalists with an income of more than a lakh of rupees. Yet the class divergence may be evidenced from Ceylon. In the British civil service the salaries vary from £150 to £3,000 a year. In the Ceylon public service the salaries range from Rs. 420 to Rs. 30,000. Since direct taxation is much lower in Ceylon, the divergences in the net figures are even greater. It must be remembered that the Ceylonese civil servant is able to obtain a substantial dowry and is thus a capitalist as well as an employee.

Against the factors which make for disintegration must, however, be balanced the factors which integrate. We are often reminded, very properly, that Hindu culture was highly developed when the ancient Britons were barbarians. In spite of the vast changes of the past 300 years that culture has been retained by the Brahmans and has been revitalized under nationalist impulses. Nor is it now a monopoly of the Brahmans. Though they alone formerly had access to the sacred texts, their essential elements spread through Hinduism and nursery stories. European scholarship and university education have helped to widen the appeal of the texts themselves. Also, Indian culture has always secured wide expression through craftsmanship, art, music, and dancing. This culture is not strictly Hindu, for it was profoundly influenced by Greek, Arabic, and Persian in the broadest possible sense. Indeed, the Mughul Empire through its employment of

Hindu craftsmen, artists, musicians, and dancers made it more catholic and broadened its appeal. It is, of course, true that the illiterate villagers have a very small share in it, but this is true of all countries, and it is closely related to the traditions and superstitions of the villages in Muslim areas as in Hindu and Buddhist areas.

English education has had a smaller cultural influence than Macaulay and the Whigs had contemplated, for it caused a class divergence far greater than the Mughul Empire and dealt with ideas which were totally unrelated to the experience of the mass of the population. It has been an integrating factor, however, for it has created a politically conscious class speaking the same language and sharing common ideas. That it has also created communalism is incidental, for communalism arises from the application of common western ideas to the complex Indian society.

II

COMMUNALISM

COMMUNALISM is commonly thought of in terms of the Hindu-Muslim conflict which resulted in the separation of Pakistan from India. It should, however, be regarded as an emanation of the diversity of the Indian peoples in all its forms. It is in fact the product of the impact of western political ideas on the social organization of the Indian peoples. Wherever there is social differentiation communalism appears in some form or another. Western political ideas assume that the population is fundamentally united. It need not be entirely homogeneous, but it does assume that any political problem will be examined from the angle of its effect on the whole population. Society in any country is comprised of groups or communities, based on history, culture, language, religion, education, class, employment, locality, recreation, and so on. For instance, a person may be a Welshman, English-speaking, a Baptist, a Cambridge graduate (of Gonville and Caius), an income-tax payer, a native of Denbigh, an inhabitant of Birmingham, a member of the National Union of Teachers, and a member of the Edgbaston Golf Club. In respect of each of these characters he exhibits a patriotism which causes him to approach any political problem from the point of view of himself and his 'community'. In that sense he is a communalist. On the other hand, he has also a wider patriotism as a British subject and a citizen of the United Kingdom. Precisely how he solves the conflict, if there is a conflict, is largely a personal question; but taking the population as a whole there is a sufficient national patriotism to enable questions of a national order to be solved by argument about its national implications. This may involve a party system which is in large measure a product of communal or sectional interests. We should guess that our English-speaking Welshman, for instance, was one of the 'intellectuals' of the Labour Party, whereas if he were a bank manager and a member of the Church of England we should probably find him voting Conservative. The essential point is, however, that almost invariably a national problem is examined from a national angle, even though each individual cannot avoid a bias due to his sectional interests.

The position in the three countries is not fundamentally different. The national patriotism, being recent and in large measure a product of British rule, by reaction or otherwise, is weak; and this weakness is emphasized by the illiteracy of the great mass of the population. Those sectional interests which arise from race, caste, language, and religion, being founded on ancient and deep-seated traditions, are strong. Interests arising from class are comparatively weak because, though in many cases (e.g. among the peasants or ryots) they are ancient, the social conditions have not until recently given birth to the idea of class solidarity, an idea which has come in from the West.

Nor must it be assumed that communalism is essentially an Indian characteristic: it necessarily arises where a sectional interest is stronger than the national interest, and there have been other examples even in the British Commonwealth. In Canada, at least until 1867, the essential political conflict was between the French of Lower Canada, or Quebec, and the English of Upper Canada, or Ontario. This conflict was based in part on 'race', for though the English and the French in Europe have a common ancestry and are not endogamous in principle they had developed different traditions which are racial in the Indian sense of the term. It was also a conflict of language, which was indeed the medium in which the different traditions were expressed and carried on. It was, thirdly, a conflict of religion, for the French were mainly Roman Catholic and the English mainly Protestant. Though the Durham Report of 1839 is more famous for its advocacy of responsible government, its principal diagnosis was that the political troubles of Canada were due to 'the conflict of races', and its principal recommendation was that the two Canadas should be fused in order that in due course the English should swamp the French. In the United Province of Canada created in 1841 in consequence of the Report the French showed no signs of being swamped; on the contrary they showed themselves signally tenacious of their existence. Indeed the equality of representation which was accorded to the English minority proved of great assistance to the French when they became the minority and a source of complaint to the English, who demanded 'representation by population'. Statesmen on both sides, especially Baldwin and Lafontaine in the earlier period and Macdonald and Cartier in the later, strove to create a common national tradition which led eventually to the establishment of the Dominion of Canada, with the culture of Quebec protected by a federal constitution which the efforts of eighty years have failed to modify substantially. Though Canadian politics are generally fought on national issues, the French are still a 'minority' in the Indian sense, and constant attention has to be paid to French-Canadian interests and susceptibilities by Canadian statesmen of all parties.

Ireland supplies another example. Though united with Great Britain in 1800, no national sentiment developed throughout the new United Kingdom. The economic advantages which had accrued to Scotland under the Act of Union of 1706 did not accrue to Ireland under the Act of Union of 1800. There was therefore no incentive for the Irish, as there was for the Scots, to consider themselves Britons. The Roman Catholics, who as always were under much stronger religious influences than the Protestants and much more a 'community' in the Indian sense, found themselves under disabilities that the obstinacy of George III prevented the Government from removing. The distinction of religion was also a distinction of class, for the landowners

were mainly Protestants and the peasants were mainly
Catholics. Thus there developed a national sentiment which
was exclusively Irish and based itself on the traditions of
Ireland, including its language, which would have died out
like Cornish but for nationalist sentiment. Attempts to treat
the problem as purely economic, by reform of the land laws,
failed because 'communalism' was too strong. Attempts to
put down Irish nationalism by repression resulted only in
strengthening nationalist sentiment by creating martyrs.
Gladstone's Home Rule plan came late but might have suc-
ceeded had it been accepted by the Parliament of the United
Kingdom. Its failure led almost inevitably to the rebellions of
1916 and 1919 and the creation of the Irish Free State.

The Hindu-Muslim conflict must not be thought of exclusively as a conflict of religious groups. The Christians
and the Sikhs have generally supported the Hindus. Moreover, the two groups are divided by other elements of discord.
Most of the Muslims belong to peoples which were once
Hindu, often of low caste and generally of low economic
status. In changing religion they did not change social and
economic status. The traders, money-lenders, and landed
peasants are usually Hindu; the labourers are often Muslim.
The brotherhood of Islam gave them a sense of prestige and
even authority which they would have lacked as depressed
or even untouchable Hindus. As Muslims they could ignore
or resent the social pretensions of the 'twice-born'; if excuse
were provided their lowly economic status, especially where
they were in the toils of Hindu money-lenders, might induce
them to combine against their economic superiors. In other
words, the Hindu-Muslim conflict is not merely an opposition of religious groups; it is also a class conflict and, in some
measure, a caste conflict.

It may be noted that in Ceylon the situation was partially
reversed. There the Moors were the shopkeepers, traders,
and money-lenders upon whom the Sinhalese villagers were
economically dependent. The only communal riots in that

country were those of 1915. They arose out of the same kind of grievance as in India, the playing of music before mosques: but the riots had a deeper economic cause, the dependence of the Sinhalese villagers on the Muslim money-lenders and traders which induced the former to take an opportunity to pay off old scores. The Muslims of India were so intransigent that Pakistan had to be created: the Muslims of Ceylon, while demanding communal representation and special privileges as a coherent minority, have nevertheless worked with the Sinhalese for self-government.

There have been other conflicts both in India and in Ceylon. There is ample record of caste controversies in India long before there began a struggle for political power.[1] Even in Ceylon and among the English-educated a caste symbol is the equivalent of the English boy's 'Jackie Jones is a fool like a donkey on a stool'; and in Jaffna there has been bloodshed because it was proposed to cremate a member of a depressed class in a cemetery reserved for caste Hindus. It has been alleged both in south India and in Jaffna that the policy of prohibiting alcoholic liquor has grown less through anxiety for social reform than through the growing wealth and influence of the toddy-tappers. As soon as political power began to be transferred to Indians the depressed classes or 'scheduled castes' began to organize themselves and to demand separate representation. In the Madras Province, where the Muslims are few, the essential conflict since 1919 has been between the Brahmans and the other caste Hindus. In delimiting constituencies in Ceylon it has been necessary to take caste as well as race into consideration.[2] Between 1931 and 1947 the only disturbances at elections were in constituencies where caste conflict was strong.

The fact that the Hindu-Muslim conflict does not extend to Ceylon enables us to see clearly that religion is not the only

---

[1] See, e.g., Senart, *Caste in India*, pp. 17–18, and sources there quoted.
[2] Jennings, 'The General Election of 1947', *University of Ceylon Review*, vol. vi, no. 3.

basis of controversy. The population of the island is usually classified as Sinhalese, Ceylon Tamils, Indians, Muslims, Burghers, and Europeans. The classification is obviously illogical. The Sinhalese are mostly Buddhists but include a large number of Christians; accordingly the classification follows a fictitious race theory or (what is the same thing) a hypothetical 'mother tongue' theory. The Ceylon Tamils are mostly Hindus but include a large number of Christians; but the Indians are nearly all Tamil-speaking Hindus: hence the classification is based partly on a fictitious race or 'mother tongue' theory and partly on locality of origin. The Muslims are of course defined by religion. The Burghers are the descendants of Portuguese and Dutch settlers and are usually but not always Eurasians. The Europeans can only be described as recent immigrants from Europe who are not Burghers. The dominant factor, therefore, is 'race', i.e. recent descent.

In India the demand for Pakistan led to a demand for a Pathanistan, and in the south there was talk of a Dravidistan. More significant is the demand for the creation in the Indian Union of linguistic provinces. It is claimed that Madras Province, for instance, should be divided into four, so that the Tamils, the Telegus, the Malayalis (with or without Travancore), and the Kannadas (with or without Mysore) can each have a province. West Bengal wishes to incorporate those parts of Bihar in which Bengali is spoken. The Marathas lay claim even to Bombay, though here there appears to be a conflict between language and history.

It is therefore clear that India, Pakistan, and Ceylon are countries in which ancestral loyalties of all kinds are strong. Nationalism itself is an ancestral loyalty of exactly the same type, for it is based on common history including, usually, race, language, and perhaps religion. There are countries like the United Kingdom, the United States, Canada, and Switzerland where there are considerable elements of diversity, but none have so many such elements as India and Ceylon.

In those countries, too, the ancestral loyalty which goes by the name of nationalism has had little chance to develop because, except under British rule, and then subject to severe limitations, a national unity could not be established.

COMMUNALISM AND BRITISH RULE

The unity which British rule imposed on India, as defined in 1946, was of slow development and lasted but a short time. Except for the North-West Frontier, British India took roughly its final form under Lord Dalhousie (1848–56). The Punjab was annexed in 1849 and Oudh in 1856. The North-West Frontier Province was not formed until 1900. During the same period the relations with the Indian States were settled, more or less on the modern basis. Even when the Government of India was transferred to the Crown in 1858 and even when the doctrine of 'paramountcy' had developed, there was no real unity. The citizen of an Indian State was not a British subject, and though the Crown was able to prevent the worst types of maladministration the Raj operated indirectly through the rulers and not directly upon the State citizens.

If British India alone be considered, the unity of India may be said to date from 1858. Ninety years in the history of India is a very short period. It would be long enough for national ideas to develop if there were strong centripetal forces. The population of India was, however, so diverse in race, language, caste, and religion that the centrifugal forces were far stronger. Socially and economically most of the villages have changed little through the centuries. Pax Britannica prevented the armed forays which were once a feature of Indian life. Efficient administration enabled the worst effects of famine and flood to be overcome; but the consequent growth of population caused a fragmentation of land which seems to have reduced the standard of living. Pax Britannica removed one possible source of national unity, common defence against an external enemy. Though after 1920 each of the major groups found means to appeal to the villagers, nationalism as such was developed among the English-educated of the towns. It was in fact a product of English education, a western idea adopted by those who had access to such ideas.

Its application to India was necessarily attended with difficulties. It was a doctrine of slow growth in Europe, and it was almost invariably limited to language-groups. In its most developed form, the doctrine of self-determination of peoples, it clearly referred to such groups. But language is not the only element of division in India, nor the most important. As soon as claims to power began to be made each important 'community' began to stake claims for its members. The Muslims wanted protection against the Hindus, the Sikhs against the Muslims, and the Christians against all other religious groups. The non-Brahmans, though the most numerous, wanted protection against the Brahmans because of their historic dominance; and the 'scheduled castes' wanted protection against the caste Hindus. The Anglo-Indians and the Europeans wanted their privileges protected. The doctrine of the racial or hereditary 'mother tongue' was developed, not merely as a nationalist reaction to British rule, nor only as a lower-class reaction to the domination of the English-educated, but also by way of competition among the Indian languages—Urdu against Hindi, the Aryan languages against each other, the Dravidian languages against the Aryan languages and the Dravidian languages against each other.

All this can be explained without fanciful interpretations of British policy. It arises from the weakness of a nascent nationalism and the strength of ancient loyalties. The assertion that Britain created communalism through applying the Roman maxim of *divide et impera* is obviously false. That the policy was applied and that it strengthened communalism can be argued, though not very plausibly. Such a policy if formulated would be found in a Cabinet decision or at least in a viceregal minute. No such decision or document has been produced. Nor is it likely that a decision of this kind would be taken or, if taken, would be consistently applied. It is much easier to argue, and indeed it is in the British tradition, that policy fluctuated from Government to Government and from Viceroy to Viceroy. Until 1917 Britain had no policy relating to self-government, not even a policy against it. Lord Morley's statements, for instance, are quite inconclusive. Though in public he expressed a disbelief in its possibility, in private he was less positive, for the obvious reason that he could not foresee the social and economic development of India.

The statements of Secretaries of State and Viceroys, however, are not necessarily conclusive. There might be an unexpressed but nevertheless clear bias in administration, not directed from above, but implicit in the conditions. If so, it must have developed in the present century. If there was a bias after 1858 it was towards the Hindus, for the Muslims were thought to have given greater support to the Mutiny. The raising of the Indian Army mainly from the North-West Frontier can hardly be said—though it has been said—to be support for communalism. The strength of the Indian Army under British rule lay in the Rajputs, the Sikhs and other Punjabis, the Pathans of the Frontier, the Dogras of Kashmir, and the Gurkhas of Nepal. It was thus a polyglot army drawn from three of the four main religious groups of India. It was raised in the north-west because it was expected to fight on the Frontier, where the tribes were turbulent and whence invaders might be expected to come. It is no doubt true that the ordinary British officer found his ways to be more attuned to those of the so-called 'martial races' than to those of the caste-ridden Hindus of the east and south; but that he had any idea of preventing the formation of an Indian 'national' army is to rate his intelligence too high.

It is also true that after 1906 the activities of the Indian National Congress were not viewed with favour by the higher officials, civil and military. The ideas of the nationalist politicians were 'seditious' because they threatened to lead and often did lead to disorder, which it was the officials' job to prevent. In 1917 the doctrine of self-government by evolution was laid down officially, and there is no evidence that the officials, high or low, did anything to hinder the evolution: but a policy of self-government by evolution is not a policy of self-government by boycott, non-cooperation, and disorder. The steps necessary to prevent such forms of political action do not need to be explained by long-term policy; they were part of the day's work of governing; the officials had to govern from day to day whatever the ultimate policy might be.

Further, it is said that communal representation was adopted as part of the policy of 'divide and rule'. Ceylon experience shows that this was not so. Until 1921 there was no need to divide in order to rule, because the Governor could rule by means of his official majority. Communal representation through nomination by the Governor was in operation for the whole of the second half of the nineteenth century because that seemed the obvious and indeed the inevitable method of giving the Ceylonese a share in the government. After 1910 there was still an official majority, but a few of the members were elected communally instead of being nominated communally. From 1917 onwards the nationalist organizations, which were mainly but not exclusively Sinhalese, demanded a majority elected territorially, but they recognized that the communal minorities must be represented by communal election or nomination. This was not accorded in 1920, but it was accorded in 1924, so that the period during which the territorial members, the communal members, and the official members were balanced against each other lasted three years. The territorially elected members were in fact either as communal or almost as communal as the communally elected and nominated members. In 1928 the Donoughmore Commission found that communal representation accentuated communalism, and proposed its abolition; but they did not find that territorial representation caused communalism to disappear. 'It is almost true to say that the conception of patriotism in Ceylon is as much racial as national, and that the best interests of the country are at times regarded as synonymous with the welfare of a particular section of the people.'[1]

The conclusion seems to be that in Ceylon the introduction of communal representation, whether by election or by nomination, was a mistake; but we can so describe it because we have had experience of its consequences. It did not create communalism, because communalism existed already. It accentuated communalism, but it was introduced because communalism was already in existence. The communities were represented because the Ceylonese were represented.

Communal representation by election had the same origin in India as in Ceylon: it grew out of communal representation by nomination which was established as the only means of representing the Indian people. Communal electorates were first conceded in the Morley–Minto Reforms in 1909, and the suggestion came not from the authors of those Reforms or from the officials but from the Muslims. Much stress is laid by Indian writers on a letter from a high official quoted by Lady Minto in her *India, Minto and Morley*[2] describing the Viceroy's response as 'nothing less than the pulling back of sixty-two millions of people from joining the ranks of the seditious opposition'. The views of a high official of the Government of India are not necessarily the views of the Government of the United Kingdom. There is no evidence that the demand was instigated by the Viceroy or by anyone else. Britain did not create the opposition between the Muslim League and the Congress. In India as in Ceylon communal representation was accepted because it seemed to be in accord with the local situation. Whether it was a mistake is perhaps a matter of opinion, for it is not possible to guess what the consequences of rejection would have been. The

[1] Report of the Special Commission on the Constitution (Cmd. 3131), p. 31.
[2] Page 34.

comments of the Donoughmore Commission in Ceylon seem to be sound and they obviously had relevance to India: yet even in 1945 most of the minorities of Ceylon were asking for communal representation.

THE PROBLEM

Whether the British created or strengthened communalism is relevant to the present position only in so far as it enables us to judge whether it is an important factor now that British rule has been withdrawn. In this connexion we may note that though there have been no communal electorates in Ceylon since 1931 and though the great mass of the electors has never voted in a communal electorate, it was necessary to give communal weightage in 1947. Further, every constituency in Ceylon which had a communal majority in 1947 elected a member from that community. All the Tamil constituencies elected Tamils and seven of the nine elected members of the communal organization, the All-Ceylon Union of Tamils. All the constituencies where Indians predominated elected members of their communal organization, the Ceylon Indian Congress. Finally, it is sufficient to note that as soon as Pakistan was created there were communal disorders on both sides of the new frontiers and millions of refugees passed both ways. Evidently neither the abolition of communal electorates in Ceylon nor the removal of British rule in India, Pakistan, and Ceylon has had much effect in diminishing communalism. Indeed, it has been said that communalism has increased since Ceylonese Ministers assumed responsibility in 1931.

It is surely more consonant with the facts to regard communalism as arising from the diversity of the peoples of the three countries, the weakness of nationalism, and the strength of ancestral loyalties. British administrators have always held the view that justice or equity required them to hold the scales of administration even, to give weight even to the smallest minority. There was indeed a tendency for them to

champion the cause of the weak because they needed protection and the strong did not. Nor was it ever made clear to
them that their fundamental task was to develop a tradition
of nationalism: indeed it was not easy for them to do so, for
nationalist opinion was always in advance of official policy.
This seems to be an inevitable consequence of the doctrine
of self-government by evolution, for its acceptance at once
causes difference of opinion over the pace of evolution. These
circumstances are sufficient to explain the official attitude.
The officials did not divide in order to rule. The divisions were
there, but they did and could do little to remove them.

The question whether communalism has gained in strength
in recent years cannot be answered because nobody knows
his strength until he has occasion to use it. The gulf which
divided the Hindu from the Muslim inhabitants of a village
did not appear to be very great so long as only village affairs
were under consideration and an alien government held the
scales. The gulf was certainly in existence, for a Hindu could
not marry a Muslim or eat from the same dish as a Muslim, but
for ordinary village purposes it was irrelevant. It might become relevant if the village *panchayat* was likely to be dominated
by a Hindu majority and it would certainly be relevant if the
Government became Hindu. The introduction of representative government therefore involved a more emphatic
expression of the gulf even if it did not widen the gulf. Also,
the communal leaders necessarily took occasion to mobilize
their followers, and their propaganda would inevitably increase the strength of local feeling. Against this tendency
must be set the tendency towards unity through nationalist
propaganda, though it must be remembered that the psychological basis of nationalism was weak while that of communalism was strong.

In the main, though, the communal agitation lay in the
towns and among the English-educated. These groups had
much more at stake. The main industry for the English-
educated is government service. In India, for reasons already

given, the Hindus took more readily to English education than the Muslims; and among the Hindus the Brahmans took to it more readily than the other castes, while the scheduled castes were virtually excluded. The Indianization of the services proceeded slowly, more slowly than English education developed, so that there was intense competition for the comparatively few posts available. Nepotism is no doubt as great a social injustice in India as elsewhere, but it is also a family virtue. Consequently, when once a family obtained a footing—and it was generally a Brahman or caste Hindu family—the chances of the rest of the family in the competition were improved. Among strangers, caste and religious loyalties were alleged to play a considerable part. It is probable—and quite certain in Ceylon—that these allegations were often false and that the best candidates were chosen irrespective of communal considerations; but they were inevitably made wherever there was a concentration of officials from a particular community.

The problem grew more difficult when the prospect of political advancement seemed to suggest that appointments would be made by Indians representing majorities. The earliest demands of the Indian National Congress were not only for more Indian representatives but also for greater Indianization of the services. Sir Syed Ahmad Khan and other Muslims had already seen the dangers and had secured the establishment of the Aligarh Muslim University in 1877, but the Muslims had never secured equality of opportunity, and they therefore demanded not merely communal representation with separate electorates but also a reservation to Muslims of a proportion of places in the public services. Nor were other interests backward. It was gradually established that places in the Provincial administration must be reserved for inhabitants of the Province if suitable candidates were available, and each group, racial, religious, or language, demanded its quota.

The development in Ceylon was similar in principle

though different in detail. The Ceylon Tamils took readily to English education and their traditional industry enabled them to be successful in examinations. Under British rule, therefore, they obtained more than their proportionate share of government posts. As English education spread in the Sinhalese low-country, however, they met increasing competition from the Sinhalese. Increased representation on a numerical basis gave the Sinhalese a further advantage, with the result that the Ceylon Tamils found their privileged position endangered. Among the Sinhalese, too, differences arose. Except in the city of Kandy, where the population was comparatively cosmopolitan owing to the rise of the plantation industries, educational facilities were concentrated in the Sinhalese low-country and in the Northern Province. The Kandyans thus became a backward community. The Muslims, too, were at least as backward in Ceylon as in India.

Thus among the English-educated communalism became the expression of a group self-interest. The majority, the Hindus in India and the Sinhalese in Ceylon, could afford to be nationalists. If the British should quit they would stand to gain most. The minorities, on the other hand, stood to gain little and might actually lose. The Muslims might prefer the Hindu Raj to the British Raj, but they would not be as enthusiastic as the Hindus, and in any event they would require safeguards.

No doubt the emphasis in politics on interests, movements, traditions, and inchoate desires tends to ignore the personal element. In Ceylon it is easy to see how personalities have influenced political development. The communal problem would no doubt have been different if Sir James Pieris, Sir Ponnambalam Ramanathan, Sir Baron Jayatilaka, Mr. D. S. Senanayake, Mr. G. G. Ponnambalam, and others had held different opinions. In India, too, there have been dominant personalities: history would have been very different but for Mahatma Gandhi. Nevertheless, a politician is mainly the

slave of his environment and it cannot be argued that communalism is a politicians' product. No doubt it would have
been less serious if they had been wiser, and history will probably resolve that the Indian National Congress played its
hand unskilfully after 1939, but communalism has deep roots
which cannot easily be eradicated, and they were not planted
by politicians.

III

EDUCATION

INCIDENTAL references have already shown that politically and sociologically the educational system plays a more important part in Asia than in the United Kingdom. In the United Kingdom we have 'educated our masters', or at least given them nine years' teaching in elementary schools. In Ceylon, where there has been adult franchise since 1931, there are still many illiterate electors;[1] and many more, though technically literate, cannot read or write fluently because their periods of school education, usually four or five years, have been too short to make them fully literate in languages so complex as Sinhalese and Tamil. In undivided India the percentage of literacy in 1931 was 9·6, though in 1941 it was believed to have reached 14·6. Since the percentage of literacy among Muslims was 6·4 in 1931, it may be presumed that Pakistan has a lower literacy rate than India as now defined. In both India and Pakistan the percentages of people who can read and write fluently are even smaller than these figures would suggest.

Theoretically, Ceylon has compulsory education from 6 to 14, but the rule is subject to so many qualifications that, as the Special Committee on Education remarked in 1943, 'compulsory education is not compulsory'. In 1946, with a population between 5 and 14 of approximately 1,600,000, the number of children at school was 933,358 or about 58 per cent.; but these include a small number (perhaps 40,000)

[1] The 1946 figures, relating to persons over the age of 4 years, are:

Literate: m., 2,170,700; f. 1,182,000. Illiterate: m., 926,700; f., 1,520,300.

Or in percentages (Literates):

Males, 70·1; females, 34·3; males and females, 53·4.

The number of illiterates has increased, though the proportion has diminished, since 1921.

under school age and a large number (perhaps 60,000) over the compulsory age. It is probable, therefore, that about half the children of school age are at school. The deficiency is due to a comparatively small number (commonly assessed at 100,000) who have had no schooling at all, and a very much larger number who enter school at 6 or 7 and leave at 10 or 11. The latter number includes most of the girls.

Undivided India showed the same tendencies more emphatically. In 1931 literacy among males was 15·6 per cent., while among females it was 2·9 per cent. Among the Muslims literacy among females was only 1·5 per cent., so that the percentage must again be much lower in Pakistan than in the Republic of India. In 1936-7, when the population aged 5 to 14 was estimated at 60 million, the number of children at school in undivided India was 11,985,986, or approximately 20 per cent. Even more significant was the fact that there was a progressive fall in numbers in each class. In class I there were approximately 5·1 million, in class II 2·3 million, in class III 1·7 million, in class IV 1·2 million, and in class V only 0·7 million. If this were evidence of a change in social convention it would be an encouraging sign: in fact, however, it represents a persistent tradition. The great majority of the children who go to school do not stay long enough to become genuinely literate, though they may be classed as literate for census purposes.

Literacy is not essential for democratic elections. The experienced villager is usually an intelligent person and a sound judge of character. So long as political controversies are within his field of experience he is a wiser and more sober elector than the sleek, half-educated city clerk. Nor must it be forgotten that where literacy is sufficiently widespread, as in Ceylon, the effective circulation of a newspaper is very much wider than its actual circulation. *Dinamina*, the Sinhalese newspaper, has a circulation of only 50,000 copies, while the *Ceylon Daily News* sells about 30,000 copies daily to the English-educated. It is, however, a common sight to see

Dinamina being read to a group of listeners who, by reason of the fact that all their knowledge comes from listening unless it is within their own experience, are extremely good listeners. It is nevertheless true that the great majority of the electors of Ceylon can have little knowledge of the world outside their own very restricted experience. They tend to be influenced by personal considerations, family influence, religion and caste, vulgar display of wealth, and other irrelevant factors.

Nor does a little education, such as most of the vernacular-educated exhibit, improve matters greatly. It is generally just sufficient to enable clever candidates to propagate lies and half-truths. This phenomenon is visible even in England, where every elector has had nine years' of schooling of a reasonably high quality. It is evident from the more popular newspapers that the ordinary elector can have but a muddled idea of the issues on which he is being asked to vote. In Ceylon the great mass of the electors are either illiterate or semi-literate. An analysis of the general election of 1947 shows a very consistent pattern. The Jaffna Peninsula and the estates elected candidates who emphasized communalism, and indeed in Jaffna caste was one of the main issues. In the Sinhalese areas the most backward constituencies elected 'independent' candidates who relied essentially on personal influence. The slightly less backward areas generally elected members of the United National Party who were of the same type and who emphasized their personal influence, though the personal influence of the Prime Minister and other leading members of the Party played some part. Finally, the slightly better-educated electors elected Marxist candidates not because they were Marxists but because they were able to use rash promises and vivid denunciations—though, of course, other candidates used the same methods where they could. There was, too, widespread electoral corruption, especially in the towns. Though the election became a contest between the United National Party on the one hand and the communal and Marxist groups on the other, it is impossible to say that the conflict was one of policy.

In India and Pakistan there are vast areas where not even the motor-bus is known and where a newspaper is never seen. It is impossible to believe that electors in such areas can make any choice except on personal grounds or because of specific promises of local or personal benefits. It must be remembered, too, that in many areas women are segregated from all men except those of their own family and that they are unable to take part in political discussions outside their homes.

The problem of the franchise was much discussed in Ceylon between 1928 to 1931. Under the Constitution then in operation, only 4 per cent. of the population had the franchise. The Ceylon National Congress asked for a large extension, but even they were not prepared for all adult males to be enfranchised and had not even thought of suggesting that adult females should get the vote. The Donoughmore Commission was anxious to recommend a substantial increase of self-government, but pointed out that with a 4 per cent. electorate any such extension would result in a middle-class oligarchy. The Commission examined several suggestions for drawing a line short of adult suffrage. An age qualification higher than 21 years for men was rejected because it would have disfranchised some of the then voters. A property and income qualification was rejected because the low income groups needed representation more than the others. Finally, a literacy qualification was rejected, partly because 'any real and genuine literacy test would rule out many thousands, peasants and others, who might be intelligent and suitable', partly because it would rule out the lower castes, and partly because it would be extremely difficult to organize an efficient literacy test.

The Commission therefore recommended manhood suffrage. There was little demand for womanhood suffrage, but the Commission was impressed with the high infantile mortality and the need for housing and social services. The inferior position of women was changing, and it was difficult to deny the force of the argument that the women were as competent as the men to exercise the vote. In order to avoid too sudden an increase in the electorate, the Commission recommended that women over 30 years of age be enfranchised; but when the Legislative Council debated the proposals a resolution for enfranchising the women on the same terms as the men was passed, and was accepted by the Government. Ceylon has thus had adult franchise since 1931.

There is no doubt that in the elections of 1931, 1936, and 1947 there was a great deal of corruption. It was thought to be impossible to ask an illiterate population to mark ballot papers, and so coloured ballot boxes were provided in 1931; but since the secrecy of the ballot required these to be placed behind screens, it became easy for an elector to hide his ballot paper in his banian and sell it outside to an agent of one of the candidates. In 1947, therefore, simple symbols (an elephant, an eye, a house, a bicycle, an umbrella, &c.) were allocated to the candidates and were printed on the ballot papers, which had to be marked. This stopped the selling of ballot papers, but gave emphasis to impersonation. In the towns the labour force is highly mobile, lives in overcrowded tenements, and is not easily identifiable. A careful canvass before the election discloses a large number of 'unknown' electors who can be impersonated at the poll with reasonable security. There is no such difficulty in the villages, where it is usually possible to find polling agents who can identify the voters and recognize 'foreigners'.

Clearly the legislatures face a dilemma. On the one hand the people with the lowest incomes, who are generally illiterate, are precisely those whose influence ought to be brought to bear in elections so as to compel politicians, who are almost invariably drawn from the English-educated professional classes, to pay some attention to their needs. It is particularly to be noted that most of the members of the lower castes are among those with the lowest incomes, so that any restriction of the franchise would entrench the power of the higher castes. Any such restriction would also intensify racial and religious communalism, for in the Union of India most of the Muslims, and in Ceylon most of the Indians and Kandyan Sinhalese, are in the low income groups. On the other hand adult suffrage gives rise to corruption and assists the demagogues.

The solution of this problem, to 'educate our masters', would require a long period and much expense. Even in Ceylon the erection of schools and the provision of teachers are just keeping ahead of the growth of population. In undivided India Sir John Sargent estimated that to provide basic education from 6 to 14 for all children would take 30 to 40 years and would require an annual expenditure of 200 crores of rupees (£150 million). Meanwhile a literacy campaign for adults would have to be carried on and spread over 20 years, the annual cost being another Rs. 3 crores (£2¼ million).

There are many suggestions for 'mass education' based on Russian experience; but doubt has been cast, by those who had experience of Russian regiments during the war, on the validity of the claims made by Soviet propaganda. It is indeed difficult to believe that millions of people can be made truly literate by voluntary effort. Even after nine years of elementary education 2 per cent. of English children are for all practical purposes illiterate. Five years of elementary education are necessary even to lay the foundation of literacy for the average pupil. Adults, or at least some adults, learn more quickly; but the number who can, after a day's work, attend evening classes constantly enough and long enough to be able to read and write will be small. Moreover, few of the languages of the Indian area are sufficiently furnished with reading-matter of an elementary and graded character to enable the reading habit to be acquired. Optimism is part of a politician's stock-in-trade but it is also one of his liabilities. He wants quick results, but this is a field where speed produces shoddy material.

EDUCATION AND CLASS DISTINCTIONS

According to most Indian politicians, Lord Macaulay is the principal figure in the devil's Pantheon. It is true that in his famous Education Minute of 1835 he expressed himself with his customary over-emphasis and exaggeration. Nevertheless, he was correct in his main argument, that neither Sanskrit nor the spoken languages could be used as instruments of more advanced education, and that English had to be used to bring India into contact with modern ideas. Nor was he wholly wrong in asserting that English education would filter down and enrich the vernaculars. In fact, Macaulay's influence on the development was small. English education proceeded apace not because the East India Company was persuaded by Macaulay to subsidize it, but because there was a demand for it. Until 1835 the Company had subsidized the ancient learning, but the subsidies were wasted because there was no demand for pundits qualified in Sanskrit or Persian. After 1835 the subsidies were not wasted because there was a demand for English-educated Indians. What Macaulay did —which must not be confused with what Macaulay said— was to divert funds from economically useless expenditure to economically useful expenditure.

As usual, Ceylon can correct a false historical perspective, for it had no Macaulay. The Dutch Company provided education in Sinhalese and Tamil and the British Government took over these schools. The Christian missionaries, too, provided education in the vernaculars, though they also provided English education for European and Burgher children. Not being racially minded, they did not refuse Sinhalese and Tamil children, and the demand for schools rose rapidly, with the result that the main missionary effort had to be switched from vernacular schools to English schools. The Government had no interest in English education until after the Colebrooke report of 1831, and it did not begin subsidizing missionary schools until 1842.

The demand for English education was not due to any love of English or even of the English. It was due mainly to the fact that English education enabled the Sinhalese and the Tamils, like the Burghers, to obtain posts in the government service and, at a somewhat later stage, in commercial employment. Except in the churches and the schools, there was no economic demand for vernacular education, and every ambitious parent desired his sons to have an English education, as indeed he still does. It was the more desired because it was difficult to obtain, had to be purchased, and therefore had a scarcity value. Had Macaulay been in advance of his era and urged that English education should be provided free and for everybody, his memory would be even less revered, for what everybody has nobody particularly wants, and yet he would have avoided one of the main social and political problems of the three countries.

Since English education was expensive it could be acquired only by those who could afford to purchase it. In Ceylon it was at first available only to the Burghers and the *Mudaliyar* class, whose sons were enabled to become clerks, interpreters, preachers, and teachers. They in turn were able to provide English education for their sons and nephews, brothers, cousins, and even remoter relations; for the sense of family obligation is high, and when once a single member of a family raises himself into the English-educated class the rest of the family tends to follow. Parents will make great sacrifices— mortgage whatever lands they possess and live in penury—in order to provide an English education for their eldest son, and he in turn will see that his younger brothers and even, if need be, their children have the same advantage. Such a process emphasizes the class division. Though on the margin of the English-educated class there are families in which some of the sons speak English and others do not, the division is transitional and very soon the whole family will become English-speaking. Even the daughters will learn English, for their prospects of marriage will be enhanced by this ability.

It should be emphasized, too, that in Ceylon the English-educated are English-speaking. In India the development of female education proceeded more slowly and emphasis was given to primary education in the vernaculars at an earlier stage. Consequently, English-educated Indians generally speak the vernacular at home and even among themselves. English-educated Ceylonese, on the other hand, speak English at home—though the new generation of parents is tending to speak Sinhalese or Tamil to their children —and to each other; the vernaculars are spoken to servants, petty tradesmen, labourers, and others of lower social status.

The use of English is thus a class distinction because it proves membership of a superior economic grade. In Ceylon, though not so often in India, there is also a distinction of costume, for either western dress or an equally distinct and more self-conscious 'national costume' is worn by the English-educated. In highly industrialized countries the distinction between the proletariat and the bourgeoisie cannot be drawn, either according to the definitions of the Communist Manifesto or according to any other definitions, for the gradations of income are so numerous and so small that there are numerous classes shading into each other. If the distinction be based not on the factor of wage-earning but on that of income, it is still possible to draw a distinction in agricultural countries, the peasants, labourers, and small shopkeepers being on one side of the line and the clerks, traders, and larger shopkeepers being on the other. In the three countries, but especially in Ceylon, the distinction is made evident by a change of language and dress. There are, of course, gradations in each group—the vernacular teachers, motor drivers, shopkeepers, labour contractors, &c. separating themselves from the peasants and labourers in one group and the administrative officers, landowners, and shopkeepers separating themselves from the clerks in the other.

The combination of class distinction and language barrier

is attacked from two angles. Those who dislike the class distinction necessarily criticize the language barrier; but those who dislike the language barrier do not necessarily criticize the class distinction. The great mass of the population, who at present have only vernacular education or none at all, would prefer to have English education for the reason that the English-educated classes have taken to it—to improve their economic status. Thus the whole population, as parents, desires English education. On the other hand, the mass of the population would equally welcome the compulsory use of the 'mother tongue' which they themselves use, while the keen nationalists among the English-educated would welcome the use of the 'mother tongue' for sentimental reasons: a nation, it is said, must have a national language, and English is regarded as a relic of subjection to British rule.

In the result there is a curious dichotomy in public policy. Resolutions of legislatures and political parties invariably favour the 'mother tongue', while at the same time more and more 'English' schools are being provided not merely by private enterprise but also by the Government. The politician who demands education through the 'mother tongue' also complains that there are not enough English schools in his constituency. The solution to this problem is, of course, to give the vernacular the economic status which English has hitherto enjoyed. The difficulty of adopting this principle even as an ultimate objective is, however, that none of the three countries has a common vernacular. In Pakistan the main languages are Urdu, Punjabi, Sindhi, and Bengali; in India there are very many, but thirteen languages are mentioned in the Constitution. In Ceylon Sinhalese and Tamil are the main languages. Thus, if a single 'official language' is selected—say Urdu in Pakistan, Hindi in India, and Sinhalese in Ceylon—it will be foreign to millions of people. It is true that English is foreign to even more millions, but at least it is communally impartial, whereas the choice of a local language as official language gives a preference to those who already speak it. Ceylon has the easiest task, for it could use both Sinhalese and Tamil; but since English would also be necessary for all those engaging in commerce and most of those in government service, this would require nearly all those in the better-paid posts to read and write fluently in Sinhalese, Tamil, and English.

There is, too, considerable doubt about the suitability of the local languages, as they exist at present, to express all the needs of the modern world. Not having been used in the past except for the ordinary occurrences of everyday life, they have not been developed to suit the needs of modern science, medicine, law, and technology. If they are to be used for professional purposes they must also be used for professional training, but there are no teachers competent so to use them nor books in which modern subjects can be studied. Clearly the whole course of education must be through the 'mother tongue' before it is used for professional purposes. Until lawyers, for instance, are taught through Sinhalese they cannot be expected to argue legal issues or to decide those issues in Sinhalese.

In India and Pakistan primary education is in the 'mother tongue', which may or may not be the language, or one of the languages, selected as the official language. In recent years, too, much of the secondary education is given in the same language. On the other hand higher education—which in India and Pakistan usually begins at 15 or 16—is in English. Pupils in secondary schools thus spend a great deal of their time in learning English to such a level that it can be used as the medium of instruction in the University. In Ceylon Sinhalese or Tamil is compulsory in the first five standards, which means that a student who desires secondary education must become skilled in English by the age of 11.

It is doubtful if any of the languages has yet been sufficiently furnished to enable even primary education to be as good as that which might have been obtained in English. The simple books which are used for elementary teaching in any language need to be based on much research and experience. The words must be simple and the ideas which they express must be both simple and familiar. What is more, the parent must have similar books available so that he can read to his child, and the child himself must have similar books to enable him to gain experience in reading as soon as he has learned the technique. In most of the Indian languages these books do not exist; nor can they be obtained by translating English books, for though the ideas may be simple in translation the language may become difficult.

On the other hand, it is educationally unsound and, indeed, extremely difficult to teach a child through a language which he does not speak at home. Nor are English books always suitable. The nursery rhymes, fairy stories, tales of adventure, and so on, which English boys and girls read relate to conditions with which they are familiar. They may be quite unfamiliar to oriental students. 'Pat-a-cake, pat-a-cake, baker's man, Bake me a cake as fast as you can' means nothing to those who eat rice and not wheat. 'Baa, baa, black sheep' and 'Little Bo-Peep' are unintelligible to children who have never seen sheep. Little Boy Blue allowed the sheep to go into the meadow and the cows in the corn, which is confusing to children who have never seen sheep, meadows, or corn. Unfamiliar animals and places may, of course, become familiar through stories, like the Three Bears and, indeed, the whole of fairyland; but the material available in English has far less relevance in Asia than in Europe, North America, or Australia.

Even so, the child who acquires a knowledge of English at home has an immense advantage. He is almost invariably bilingual, for he speaks the vernacular to his ayah and other servants if not to his parents. Discerning parents, in fact, insist on his learning to speak his vernacular not merely because they are nationalists but also because they believe that nationalist sentiment will require him to possess a knowledge of the vernacular. At school he will be taught through the vernacular, but the books which are read to him by his parents and which he will read for enjoyment as soon as he can will be in English. He has thus a far broader educational foundation than his vernacular-speaking neighbours, and at whatever stage the medium is changed he will find himself far better prepared. The bilingual students are, however, those from the middle classes, and so the whole educational system favours those classes. Nor is it easy to see how this advantage can be changed, except by immense effort and after a long period.

Osmania University in Hyderabad State converted most of its courses into Urdu—which is, as it happens, the language of the Muslim minority, not of the Hindu majority. To make this possible a Translation Bureau had been in existence for twenty-five years. At the end of that period it had translated 500 books. If the list of books on any particular subject be examined, however, it will be found that in none of them is there an adequate bibliography in Urdu. Also, those who know Urdu criticize the quality of the translations. The translators have no doubt possessed an adequate knowledge of Urdu, but they have not been sufficiently skilled in the subjects of the books translated to produce an adequate interpretation. To convert a complicated idea expressed in English into a complicated idea expressed in Urdu one must clearly have not only an adequate knowledge of both languages but also a complete understanding of the idea, an understanding which no ordinary graduate can be expected to possess. Professional translators are no doubt adequate for general literature, which deals with the common emotions; they are not adequate for difficult technical work. Only a really good philosopher can translate Hegel into English, because his translation must be an interpretation. The Urdu translator has to be not equally good but even better, for western philosophy has never before been expressed in Urdu.

Other Indian universities are seeking to follow the example set by Osmania, but most of them recognize that to achieve success they have to solve immense problems. Moreover, the three largest universities—Calcutta, Bombay, and Madras—draw their students from several language groups. They must either choose one language—Bengali in Calcutta, Marathi or Gujarati in Bombay, and Tamil in Madras—which will give a large minority an immense advantage, or become multilingual universities. If English must be replaced by the vernaculars, the only solution is to divide up the great universities into smaller units, and India must have a much larger number of universities, most of them speaking different languages.

The result of such a diversification must inevitably be to break up not merely the universities but also the professions, including trade and industry. In the south, for instance, there would be four language groups, Tamil, Malayalam, Kannada, and Telugu. None of these groups would have any contact with each other or with the rest of India, unless there was a common second language, say Hindi; but if Hindi were the national language the Hindi-speaking peoples of the north would become as dominant a class as the English-speaking are now. English is at least neutral, a language which all can learn on equal terms. Hindi would give a preference to some and so would be anathema to others.

The problem may be exhibited on a smaller scale in Ceylon. English is at present a common language which may be acquired by anybody who can afford English education. Indeed, the Tamils of the north have taken to it more readily than the Sinhalese of the south, and the Tamils still enjoy a disproportionate share of the government posts. If it is replaced by a local language it must be Sinhalese, which will give the majority community a dominant position. The solution suggested is to make a knowledge of both Sinhalese and Tamil compulsory; but since most of the posts available are in Sinhalese areas, this will inevitably give an advantage to the Sinhalese. Nor must it be forgotten that neither language is yet suitable for use in higher education or professional practice. Sinhalese is spoken by some 4 million people, of whom only about 250,000 belong to the middle classes. To develop a literature, academic and technical, for some 60,000 or 80,000 families would be an immensely expensive and diffi· cult task.

The use of the vernaculars for primary education has already caused social difficulties. Sinhalese people in the north have to have their children educated in the south; Tamils in the south have to send their children to Jaffna. In Colombo, where the population is mixed, parallel classes have to be formed. These classes develop communal emotions. 'Tamil boy' and 'Sinhalese boy' become terms of abuse, though when they all learned English they rarely recognized communal distinctions. If these problems are multiplied tenfold, some idea of the difficulties facing India may be obtained.

IV

CLASS DIVISIONS

THE distinction drawn by the Marxists between 'workers' and 'peasants' is politically an important one; the workers of the towns are more easily organized for political action, while the peasants of the villages, though often more economically depressed than the workers, bear their burdens uncomplainingly and peacefully. This tendency is accentuated by the fact that in large areas of the three countries there are no capitalists. In the *raiyatwari* areas of Madras, Bombay, Central Provinces, Orissa, Coorg, and Assam, in Sind, and in Ceylon, the villagers hold their lands direct from the State. In Assam and Ceylon, however, much of the land has been incorporated into estates of considerable size employing paid labour. In the *zemindari* areas of the rest of India and Pakistan there is a landlord whose weakness politically is accentuated by the fact that neither he nor any of his predecessors in title has accepted the obligations which ownership conveys, for he was a mere farmer of taxes converted into an owner by British legislation. His days are numbered, for it was the policy of the Indian National Congress and is now the policy of the Indian Government to abolish the *zemindari* system altogether.

Pax Britannica, even where broken by communal riots, has allowed the village population to multiply. Irrigation works have enabled desert areas and dry jungle to be brought under cultivation, but the increase in the cultivable land has not compensated for the increase of population. Emigration from India to Burma, Ceylon, Africa, and the West Indies has in some slight measure relieved the pressure of population. Improved methods of agriculture are not easily introduced among villagers so conservative, especially where the system of joint ownership requires collective action, and they have done little to increase the productivity of the land. The general result has been a fragmentation of the land and a lowering of a standard of living which was already appallingly low. Cash crops like tea, rubber, coconut, cotton, coffee, jute, and sugar have done something to diversify an economy based mainly on rice or wheat produced for consumption, but they are dependent on fluctuating world prices and are cultivated more often in estates than in small-holdings. The rates of wages are low because there is no shortage of labour, there is a tendency towards over-production, and most of the competing countries have similar economies.

None of the three countries appears to be rich in minerals, and industrial development, though rapid in India in recent years, is still on a small scale. Cotton and jute provide the main avenues of employment, but in 1940 the mills subject to the Indian Factories Act employed only a million workers. In 1931 there were only 2,575 towns in India, and they contained less than 40 million inhabitants.

Apart from the *zemindari* in the north, many of whom are absentee landlords, the owners of estates, who generally leave them in the hands of superintendents, and the planters themselves, who are mainly salaried employees, the rural middle class is small and the system of squirearchy does not obtain. The middle class as a whole is small and almost entirely urban. It is distinguished from the rest of the population by its English education, which breaks down caste barriers where it is available, but is in fact available only to a small minority drawn mainly from the landowning, professional, and shopkeeper classes. Incomes tend to be lower than in Europe— except in Ceylon, where the European tradition prevails— but owing to the low incomes of the labourers, peasants, and industrial workers the spread is very wide.

This spread may be illustrated from Ceylon, where in fact the great extremes of India do not exist. In 1946 the great mass of the population was living in families whose gross income did not exceed Rs. 25 per mensem, whereas there were

3,903 individuals whose net or taxable incomes exceeded Rs. 20,000 per annum. In the government service at the present time the lowest salaries paid are Rs. 420 per annum, while some of the permanent secretaries receive Rs. 30,000 per annum. The middle classes of Ceylon are in fact divided into two groups, a division so emphatic that the term 'middle class' is often limited to the lower. The one includes the clerks, traders, and others of similar status who have left school at 17 or 18 years of age and whose incomes tend to range between Rs. 100 and Rs. 200 per mensem. The other includes the staff officers, university teachers, lawyers, doctors, and others who have graduated and who generally enjoy salaries varying from Rs. 300 to Rs. 1,000 per mensem. The gap between Rs. 200 and Rs. 300 is not entirely unfilled, but if numbers were plotted against incomes the curve would sag between those figures. The division between the two groups is socially very marked. Membership of the upper group is, for instance, indicated by the ownership of a car.

It will be seen that the class groupings are much more clearly marked than in England, where there is a slow gradation from the very poor to the very rich, the numbers falling as incomes rise. In Ceylon and Pakistan, and to a somewhat less degree in India, there are three almost separate income groups —the workers and peasants, the clerks, and the staff officers— though it must be remembered that the workers and peasants themselves are divided into three groups of equal status, the urban workers, the estate workers, and the peasants. This grouping is not very different from that in existence in Europe in the first half of the nineteenth century, when Karl Marx made his analysis. Nor is it very different from the grouping in eastern Europe to-day.

Class consciousness must clearly be strong, especially in Ceylon, where the classes are so clearly marked. The workers wear the cloth, live mainly on rice, speak the vernacular only, and inhabit houses built of kadjan or mud and wattle. The members of the lower-middle-class group wear coat and trousers, eat a little meat, speak English (though not very well), live in little brick or kabuk houses, and employ a young servant. The members of the upper-middle-class group wear European dress, eat European food, speak fluent and correct English, live in substantial bungalows, employ two or more servants, and own cars.

With comparatively few exceptions the politically conscious groups are to be found among the English-educated. The Indian National Congress obtained strong support from the Hindu villagers, but it was a quasi-religious movement dependent on the emotional appeal of Mahatma Gandhi. The Muslim League, too, capitalized the brotherhood of Islam for political purposes. In Ceylon, where adult franchise has been in operation since 1931, elections have been fought mainly on local and personal issues, and it cannot be said that the villagers have had much consciousness of a wider responsibility.

It is, however, obvious that the class divisions provide a fruitful field for left-wing politics. The leaders who claim to speak for 'the masses' are almost invariably graduates from the middle class. In Ceylon in particular most of them were educated in England. Oppressed by the penury of the great mass of the population, some university students and others of middle-class origin are easily persuaded that a social revolution is the only solution. They were supported in their views by the propaganda of the Indian National Congress and the nationalist bodies in Ceylon alleging that British rule was designed to secure 'imperialism' or 'economic exploitation of the masses'. In their opinion political independence without a social revolution is a mere substitution of 'brown capitalism' for white. In fact, they say, since it is inconceivable that the white capitalists would give up their tribute without a struggle, the independence granted is a fake, a deal between the white capitalists and the brown to enable both to continue their exploitation. Genuine independence will come when the workers and peasants take matters into their own hands; but revolutions being not mass movements of all workers and peasants but movements by the urban proletariat, there must first be a dictatorship of the proletariat. What is to happen after that is not clearly defined, for the problem in the three countries is the same as that in eastern Europe. If the peasants' land is to be 'collectivized' the peasants will vote for the capitalists and will not support the revolution.

Communism of this type is obviously a theory of the English-educated derived not from experience of Asian conditions but from the reading of Communist literature in English. That literature is not, however, unanimous. For some, Marshal Stalin is the greatest living expositor and the Soviet Union the example of Marxism in action. This gives rise to the orthodox or Stalinist Communist Party. For others, Stalin has been guilty of deviation by enunciating the theory of Socialism in one country, while the Soviet Union is a bureaucracy which bears witness to the seizure of power by irresponsible elements. The Asian countries must share in the great revolution which will in due course sweep the world as Marx foretold. This gives rise to the Bolshevik-Leninist or Trotskyist party. Ceylon, which is always prodigal in organizations, goes farther by having two Trotskyist bodies: one is commonly referred to as L.S.S.P. and the other as B.S.P. Ideologically there is no difference between them, but in practice the former is more 'opportunist' than the latter and has in fact been accused by the Stalinist Communist Party of approving by its actions if not by its ideology parliamentary action instead of revolution, though all three parties are represented in Parliament and take part in parliamentary action. The B.S.P. seems to be organically connected with the Fourth Trotskyist International, and it makes greater play with its ideology.

'The masses' for whom these contending factions claim to speak have no notion whatever of the rival ideologies. Dialectical materialism means as little to them as the Quantum Theory. What they do know is that the parties support radical measures for the raising of incomes and the provision of social services. One or other of them supports every strike—sometimes to the embarrassment of the strikers—and makes demands which compel the Government to side with the employers, thus proving that the Government is a façade for the dictatorship of the brown capitalists. Their strength cannot be determined except in Ceylon, where alone elections have been held on adult franchise. There, the three parties were strong enough to win most of the seats in the low-country south of Colombo, where the urban population predominates and the villagers are more sophisticated. Islam may be strong and cohesive enough in Pakistan to prevent the problem from arising. In India the alinement of parties is not yet clear, for the Indian National Congress combined in the struggle against 'imperialism' the great capitalists of Bombay and Calcutta and the humble followers of Mahatma Gandhi. It is, however, significant that the Government of India has found it necessary to take repressive measures against Communists. In Ceylon, where no such measures are in operation, the Indian National Congress and the Government of India are hotly attacked as the lackeys of imperialism.

The fact is that politics in all three countries are still a middle-class affair, though in Ceylon the English-educated have to appeal and in India they will soon have to appeal to working-class voters. Even the trade unions are political instruments, managed by middle-class officers (who find management not unprofitable), and concerned with conditions of employment only so far as agitation produces political results. Each group—including in India the Congress—has its own trade unions, whose membership fluctuates violently according to political conditions.

For the present, the key to the situation is held by the lower middle class. More numerous but less influential than the upper middle class, it has exhibited a tendency to move to the left. Consisting mainly of persons with comparatively low fixed incomes, it has been seriously affected by the post-war inflation, and it has developed a strong enough character to resent the flaunting of wealth by the more favoured class. Though it would be among the first to suffer if 'the revolution' really occurred it has shown a tendency to support the left-wing parties. The comparative success of those parties in Ceylon was almost certainly due to the support given by the lower middle class after a series of strikes in which both the mercantile clerks and the Government Clerical Service were supported by the left-wing parties.

It is, however, dangerous to generalize, for conditions in the three countries are too fluid to allow conclusions to be drawn. The Muslim League, at least as it was when it was led by Mr. M. A. Jinnah, is far too strong in Pakistan to give rise to serious political, as distinct from economic, problems in the near future. In India the Congress has not yet split into its component parts. Only in Ceylon are conditions becoming stable. There, adroit management by the Prime Minister, and maladroit controversies among the left-wing parties, have created a stable right-wing Government. The United National Party won 42 seats in a House of 101. It was, however, consistently supported by some 20 Independents, and it has now incorporated the Tamil Congress, which had fought the election of 1947 against the United National Party as a communal party. The present Government has therefore a solid majority of at least 40 votes, a number so large that even personal controversies, which develop so easily in Asia, are unlikely to endanger its strength. Its chance of remaining in office until the next election in 1952 is therefore high.

V

RESPONSIBLE GOVERNMENT

IT is unlikely that for some time to come any of the Asian countries of the Commonwealth will evolve new political forms. Though their potential may be great their present capacity for innovation in any field of culture is small. In politics, in any case, they have had no opportunity to invent and experiment: for, except in the States, where for the most part British power helped to maintain a primitive though (generally) benevolent autocracy, their Constitutions were made in England. Though Indians were associated with the Simon Commission in 1929, were summoned to the Round Table Conferences, and had some influence on the Government of India Act, 1935, the essential decisions were taken in London; and the probable criticisms of Mr. Winston Churchill had more effect on the drafting than the probable reactions of the Indian peoples. Not until 1943 was anybody in Ceylon asked to produce constitutional proposals.

On the other hand, during the twentieth century there was increasing association of Indians and Ceylonese with the machinery of government. The machinery was made in England, but the number of people exported from Britain to work it was very small. In Ceylon in 1939 effective power was vested in the last resort in the Governor and the Secretary of State for the Colonies, but the laws were passed in a legislature consisting of fifty-four Ceylonese, four unofficial Europeans with voting rights, and three European officials without voting rights. This particular legislature had been established in 1931, but there had been a Ceylonese majority in the legislature since 1924. Seven of the ten Ministries were controlled by Ceylonese committees over each of which a Ceylonese Minister presided, and some of these Ministers had been continuously in office since 1931. The financial policy of the island was determined by a Board of Ministers in which there were three European officials as well as the seven Ministers, but the officials had no vote. In the 'civil service', which corresponds to the administrative class in Britain, there were in 1939 only 49 Europeans, while in other branches of the public service the Europeans were few and were becoming progressively fewer. It had been settled since 1934 that no non-Ceylonese was to be appointed to the public service except after an affirmative vote of the State Council. Though the Governor's reserved powers were large, he rarely used them except to settle trivial matters in dispute like the rights of public servants to leave overseas.

The position in India was proportionately much the same. The failure of the States to execute Instruments of Accession had prevented the federal system of the Act of 1935 from being brought into operation; but in the Provinces effective power was in the hands of responsible governments and elected legislatures, subject to powers of control by the Governors which could rarely be used. The European members of the Indian Civil Service were few in number, though, since most of them were derived from an earlier stage in the political evolution and had had long experience of India, they were generally concentrated near the top. By 1947 the Service had been sufficiently indianized to enable the Provisional Government to run the risk of dismissing the lot and replacing them by Indians. Pakistan found greater difficulty in staffing its higher posts, since the number of Muslims in the Indian Civil Service was relatively small, but Pakistanis could be appointed to most of the key posts and the majority of the lower ranks.

It follows that the change to independence in 1947 and 1948 was no revolution. In Ceylon, it is true, a new Constitution came into operation in 1948; but it was a mere modification of the transitional Constitution which came into operation in 1947 and which left substantial powers in the hands of the King's representatives. It had been drafted in such a way as to make these powers easily removable. It was, in fact, a Constitution providing for complete self-government, but with qualifications inserted in such a manner that they could easily be removed. Independence was thus achieved in two steps, the first being taken with the knowledge that the second would be taken sooner or later and with the intention, on the part of the Ceylonese, that it should be sooner rather than later. The new Indian Constitution, though republican in form, is essentially British in texture, and most of its provisions bear witness to the conflicts of English constitutional history. Pakistan is being governed under a transitional Constitution formed by modifications of the Government of India Act, 1935.

Thus India, Pakistan, and Ceylon are being governed under Constitutions which are essentially British in their context and texture. India and Ceylon can amend their Constitutions as they please and the Constituent Assembly of Pakistan can, if it wishes, branch into new and unexpected fields of political science. All three countries have, nevertheless, learned the principles of democracy under British tutelage. It is inconceivable that there should be any fundamental change in this generation. Indians, Pakistanis, and Ceylonese were governed under the control of Britain for more than a century; they have exercised powers under Constitutions of British manufacture for nearly a generation; they have taken the initial steps as independent countries under documents whose principles, at least, were laid down in London; each of them has a government responsible to its legislature after the manner of British Cabinet government.

There are, however, other reasons. However autocratic the governments may have been, their modes of operation and even the principles on which they operated were fundamentally those of the British Constitution. The Governor or Governor-General had powers which no King of England since Charles I had claimed: but the day-to-day administration of the departments of government followed the practices of Whitehall. Even more important was the fact that the laws were founded on English law, except in Ceylon, where the Roman-Dutch Law was moulded by English judges so as to look startlingly like the common law. The legislation passed presupposed the fundamental assumptions on which the legislation of the United Kingdom was based. It seemed natural to assume the freedom of the press, the right of public meeting, the right of free speech, and so on; and when these rights were cut down in the interest of public order, it was done selfconsciously and apologetically.

Nor can it be forgotten that every year thousands of undergraduates, among whom the Indian National Congress obtained its strongest support, were reading books on the British Constitution and English constitutional law. Burke, John Stuart Mill, Austin, Bagehot, Bryce, and Dicey were 'prescribed texts', which were read by some and sampled by many. Bagehot and Dicey were among the books translated into Urdu by Osmania University, but elsewhere they were read in English. English constitutional history, the struggles of the barons against the King, the conflicts between King and Parliament, the battle for freedom of speech, the development of democracy, were almost as well (or as badly) known in India as in England. Ceylon was even more anglicized, for until 1942 all undergraduates read for London external examinations. The constitutions of other countries were not ignored, but they were studied through the English language and through English eyes, generally in the smaller and less accurate cram-books which gave snippets about the United States, France, and Germany. For academic purposes the Constitution which really mattered was the British Constitution, not because it was the best or the most interesting, but because India and Ceylon were tied to Britain and the subject was 'prescribed'.

University text-books were read by those who wanted to pass examinations, and the passing of examinations is one of the two great industries of the East because it leads to the second great industry, the government service. But in the environment which both the Congress and the Communist parties created, young men and women read more than their text-books. They were all what the planters called 'anti-British', but they read British books. Few knew any European language other than English, and of the books in English nine-tenths, or perhaps ninety-nine hundredths, came from Britain. Even those who did not read books read the newspaper articles written by university graduates and failed B.A.s, who read the books. Generally they were written by the intellectuals of the Labour Party—Laski, Cole, Pritt, and the rest. They were analyses and criticisms of the British Constitution and British social and economic life. The yellow backs of Mr. Victor Gollancz were on every bookshelf.

The Ceylonese politicians, achieving independence peacefully and by persuasion, had no reason to pretend. They wanted the British Constitution extended to Ceylon because they knew a great deal about it and little of any other. The Declaration of 1943, under which the Constitution of 1947 was drafted, actually used the phrase 'responsible government'; but the Ceylonese would have chosen responsible government even if there had been no such provision. They knew that under responsible government Ceylonese ministers would be responsible to a Ceylonese Parliament, an idea which seemed to them, after 450 years of foreign rule, to be admirable. There was, too, a more solid but less persuasive reason. In so far as it understood any system at all, the populace understood the British system. The British system might work: no other stood any chance of success.

In India the position was more complicated. The Congress had been in rebellion against British rule, though it had used the methods popularized by Mahatma Gandhi. Its members would therefore prefer not to follow British precedents. The United States and Eire, which had rebelled against British rule, might supply better examples. Besides, India had a minority problem which could be solved, in the view of the

Congress, by a Bill of Rights of the American type. India being a vast country, formed of very different Provinces, had to have a federal Constitution. On the other hand, the British Constitution was understood and some at least of its essential principles had been in operation in India. British India already had, on paper, a federal Constitution of British type. There was nothing fundamentally opposed to a Bill of Rights in the British Constitution. All that was required was that Dicey's principles be enacted as law.

The solution was not difficult. India would become a 'sovereign democratic republic', repudiating the Crown of the United Kingdom and thus bearing witness to the years of antagonism to British rule. It would have a federal Constitution with a distribution of powers based on the Government of India Act, 1935. It would have not only a Bill of Rights but also 'Directives of Social Policy', like Eire. But it would also have responsible government. The elected President and the Governors of Provinces would not represent the King, but they would in fact be constitutional monarchs.

Pakistan has so far done no more than draft its 'Aims and Objects', which tell us little about the form of government. Pakistan is to be a 'sovereign independent State'; it is to be a federation; fundamental rights are to be guaranteed. There is, however, little doubt that responsible government will be chosen.

Before 1947 the view was often expressed that the institutions of the West could not be transplanted in the East. Men who, as collectors, knew the people of their districts better than any city-bred Congress-wallah, said that India, the real India, had not changed in a thousand years and was not suited to democratic institutions. Attention was called to communal divisions and the caste-system, both deeply rooted in the social life of India. Emphasis was laid on the family organization, which made nepotism a virtue, and to the social conventions which excused if they did not justify corruption. It may be that with many the wish was father of the thought, and that with others the explanation was designed to reject Indian aspirations without antagonizing Indian opinion; even so, it must be confessed that the extension of responsible government to Asia is a new experiment whose success cannot be guaranteed.

We must beware of assuming that the incidents of responsible government must everywhere be the same, or that the conventions of Britain must be repeated. Responsible government is not the same in Britain, Canada, Australia, New Zealand, South Africa, and Eire; still less is it the same in the countries of Europe which have adopted it. Its essence is that a Government is chosen from or elected by a majority in the legislature. It need not be a party majority; it may be a coalition of parties or a collection of 'King's friends' held together by mutual interest or patronage or corruption. There need not be an organized opposition, and if there is it need not be an alternative government. Nor need there be collective responsibility so long as there is responsibility and the government is prepared to resign when it loses the confidence of the legislature—though it may be that resignation will be followed merely by a reorganization with a slightly different personnel. Experience has no doubt suggested that responsible government works best in the country of its origin; but it cannot be suggested that it will not work elsewhere with a different set of conventions.

The major difficulty in Asia is the survival of communalism based on race, religion, or caste. It may be noted that the House of Commons was not in origin a body representing a homogeneous population divided for convenience into more or less equal territorial constituencies. 'One man, one vote, one value' is a recent doctrine, not imported into the law until 1885 and not carried out completely until 1948. Until 1832 the 'communities' were represented equally, whatever their size—two knights for each shire and two burgesses for each borough. Nor is there any reason why the 'communities' should be territorial. If the population is socially organized into 'communities' based on race (i.e. language groups, or groups based on other socially inherited conventions), religion, or caste there can be no fundamental objection to their representation as such. The complaint against communal representation as Asia understands it is that few actions of a government or a legislature are concerned with the communities as such. There are some. The question of language, whether as medium of instruction or as medium of government, is clearly one of them, and it is a burning question in Asia. If emphasis is given to Hindi in India or Sinhalese in Ceylon those whose home language is Tamil will suffer economically. All the cultural activities of the Government fall into the same category. There can be little doubt that in Ceylon the Buddhist majority has used its power to benefit the Buddhist temples and that the non-Buddhist taxpayer has to subsidize the Buddhist religion—an accusation which is not met by pointing out that under the British the non-Christian taxpayer subsidized Christian schools and, indirectly, Christian missions. It must also be remembered that 'culture' may have a wide connotation. There are, for instance, three types of indigenous medicine in Ceylon—Sinhalese, Tamil, and Muslim—all of which claim subsidies from the State and all of which complain of the large sums spent on what is significantly described as 'western' medicine.

It is, however, true that for the most part communalism is irrelevant to government. Also, it may be demonstrated by experience as well as by reason that communal electorates increase communalism. The member who is elected to represent a communal group thinks it his duty, in season and out of season, to urge the claims of his community. He tests a proposal not by its effect on the nation but by its effect on his community. Indeed he must do so, if he wishes to keep his seat. It is hard enough, as Burke discovered, to be member for Bristol and at the same time to treat each question broadly on its merits. It is even harder to be a communal representative and to rise above communalism. It is necessary to avoid communal electorates, but where communal divisions are so ancient and so profound it is quite impossible to take communal considerations out of politics.

Ceylon has adopted a system of territorial representation with a system of weightage and a method of delimitation which pays attention to the distribution of racial, religious, and caste groups. The problem of India has become easier through the creation of Pakistan. Millions of Muslims have become citizens of a country whose Constitution will begin: 'In the name of Allah, the Beneficent, the Merciful'. Millions of Muslims who remain in India can appeal for protection, in the name of Allah, to a neighbouring country. Those Sikhs and Hindus who remain in Pakistan know that they have powerful friends to the south. Even so, it is doubtful whether the Congress members who dominated the Indian Constituent Assembly were not too optimistic in believing that they could abolish communal representation and reservation of seats at once.

The difficulty of working responsible government where communal ideas dominate lies in the permanence of the division between majority and minority and therefore between government and opposition. It is no longer true in Britain that debates influence votes, except where a 'free vote' is allowed, or that a Government with a majority runs a risk of defeat in the House of Commons. If it can avoid a split in its party it can carry every measure. What is important in Britain is not that the Government can be defeated in the House but that it can be defeated at a general election. In Asia, on the other hand, a communal government might run some risk of defeat in the legislature on issues which did not rally its communal supporters to it, but no risk of defeat at the polls where the communal appeal was dominant. If this were so the minority could never hope to influence the policy of the Government or to form a Government. The extraordinary responsiveness to public opinion in the United Kingdom of a Government which possesses a huge majority arises from its knowledge that a small 'swing' of opinion at the next election would cause it to lose its majority. If a majority in India or any of its States were based on race, religion, or caste it would run no risk of such a defeat.

It may be that in some States of the Indian Union such a system will operate. In Hyderabad, for instance, the Muslim minority has had control for so long that the Congress was essentially a Hindu organization. It was able to assume power only through armed invasion by the troops of the Indian Union. The boot being now on the other foot it seems probable that for some time to come the Muslims will be a minority in opposition. Again, in Madras caste feeling is so strong that the Brahmans may be forced into the position of a permanent minority. Taking the Union as a whole, however, it seems probable that the creation of Pakistan has transferred the Hindu-Muslim conflict from the centre of political controversy to its periphery.

It is also important that in the later phases of British rule communalism was in large measure a struggle for power. As responsibility was being transferred from British to Indian and Ceylonese hands there was a scramble for a share in the succession. In India the Muslims and in Ceylon the Tamils whipped up communal enthusiasm in order to secure special protection from the British and an entrenched position in the new order. The battle being now ended there is some prospect that communalism will become no more than a minor issue in politics. It would revive only if communalism became strong among the majority through excessive development of religious enthusiasm. The Hindu Mahasabha is a potential danger to the stability of India, as the assassination of Mahatma Gandhi showed, because it desires to keep religion in the forefront of politics. The Sinhala Mahasabha in Ceylon, on the other hand, is not an organization of Buddhist enthusiasts but an attempt to exploit communalism for personal power and prestige which is likely to fail precisely because it arouses no religious enthusiasm.

On the whole, then, communalism seems unlikely to obstruct the smooth operation of responsible government. It certainly cannot be ignored; some modification of the strict territorial principle as now applied in Britain seems inevitable; communal support has to be taken into consideration in choosing candidates, for even in Ceylon no candidate (except, very rarely, on the extreme left) stands much of a chance in a constituency unless he belongs to the race, religion, and caste of the majority; some sort of communal representation has to be provided in the Cabinet. If these conditions are satisfied there is no reason why differences of race, religion, and caste should lead to any breakdown of responsible government.

Strangely enough, the class divisions due to westernization are much more dangerous. The condition of the ordinary villager has changed little in a thousand years, but in all parts of Ceylon and in most parts of India and Pakistan the development of omnibus services has created a new sophistication, a new series of economic needs, a new complex of ideas of right and wrong. Where education is widely spread, as in Ceylon and the southern Provinces of India, common men are reading vernacular newspapers and are beginning to ask themselves, in oriental language, 'When Adam delved and Eve span, who was then the gentleman?' There are, indeed, gentlemen. They are city-bred merchants and manufacturers, university-trained civil servants and 'experts' who ride about in ostentatious cars, clothe their wives and daughters in magnificent sarees, load their female relatives with costly and flamboyant jewels, and flount their wealth on the race-courses where labourers venture their hard-earned rupees. On the one hand, there is abject poverty; on the other hand, ostentatious wealth. There is material here for revolutionary communism. Its followers have as much understanding of Marxism as they have of the Gold Standard; but they do understand that it is against the landlords and the bosses and that it seeks to abase the pretensions of the mighty.

Even more important is the class of clerks and shop-assistants, the frustrated nationalists and failed B.A.s, who set out on the road to wealth and power but fell by the wayside through shortage of funds, inadequacy of general education, lack of ability or—reasons more commonly given—bad luck, an unfortunate horoscope, lack of influential friends, or the malignancy of examiners. They read the penny pamphlets, subscribe to inflammatory newspapers, listen to or even make speeches in public places, and help to rouse the masses—with a long 'a'—to a realization of social injustice.

The one group does not understand political democracy except as a means by which the mighty increase their incomes. The other repeats the phrases of the Communist Manifesto and regards political democracy as a concession by the capitalists to keep themselves in power and the people in subjection. Neither can form the basis of a political opposition: and, since the great mass of the population truly has little to lose but its economic chains, it tends to form a real opposition. The process is more evident in Ceylon than in India and Pakistan, for popular franchise has been in operation for nearly twenty years. The backward areas continue to support their feudal lords; but the areas which have been more touched by western ideas and urbanization, like the coastal belt of the west, tend to support communism. True, it is communism with a difference: little is heard of the liquidation of private property as such, for most villagers have small plots of land. Nor has the Soviet Union as such any greater appeal than socialist Britain, for it is even more remote from the understanding of the ordinary man. The communist is supported not because he is a communist but because he is an opponent of the mighty. It makes no difference whether he is Stalinist or Trotskyite, and indeed few voters know the difference. Just as the wealthy are supported in some areas because of their prestige; so in other areas the particular brand of communism is determined by prestige of a different type. Other things being equal, for instance, one who has suffered imprisonment for his political views is preferred to one who has not: and, since the Trotskyites opposed the 'imperialist war' and went to prison while the Stalinites supported the 'war against fascism' and did not, the former are preferred because they have suffered at the hands of the mighty.

The problem of responsible government, therefore, is primarily a problem of securing such an economic development that the ordinary man finds no reason to change the form of government. Since all parties assume a rapid spread of popular education, it is also a problem of passing rapidly through the stage at which a little learning, stimulated by a virulent vernacular press, induces revolutionary movements. Whether these requirements can be satisfied needs the gift of prophecy.

VI

THE CONSTITUTION OF CEYLON

THOUGH Ceylon has had to face many of the problems of India, they have been on a smaller scale and more easily handled. There is a diversity of races—the Sinhalese, the Ceylon Tamils, the Moors, the Malays, the Burghers, the Indians, and the Europeans; a diversity of religions —Buddhism, Hinduism, Islam, and Christianity; and even some diversity of language, for Sinhalese is generally spoken in the south, outside the estates, Tamil in the north and on the estates, and English (more than in India) by the middle classes. The class division is not so acute, for the peasantry tends to be wealthier and there are few wealthy capitalists; on the other hand, the range of incomes is much greater than in western Europe. The coastal regions have been under direct European control since 1505 and the Kandyan Provinces since the Convention of 1815. British administration has been uniform throughout the country since 1833. Literates form 53 per cent. of the adult population and about 6 per cent are literate in English. About 60 per cent. of the children of school age are at school, but few (usually estimated at 100,000 or about 6 per cent.) have had no education at all. As in India a large number of children leave school at the age of 11 or 12, especially girls.

Constitutional development on modern lines began in 1910, but representative government did not begin until 1924, when only 4 per cent. of the adult population had the franchise and there were communal electorates. In 1931 these electorates were abolished, the franchise was extended to all domiciled adults, and self-government subject to considerable limitations was established. The form was peculiar, for the State Council of fifty-eight members was divided into executive committees, each in charge of a group of Departments. Each of them elected a chairman, who was appointed Minister and became a member of the Board of Ministers, which was collectively responsible to the State Council for finance but not for other aspects of government. There was thus a division of responsibility among the Governor, the Board of Ministers, the State Council, and its executive committees; nevertheless, the Board of Ministers gradually accepted wider responsibilities and behaved more and more like a Cabinet. Particularly was this so during the late war, when the island was put into a state of defence by close collaboration between the Commander-in-Chief and the commanders of the armed forces on the one side and the Board of Ministers on the other. Though there were at times disputes between the Governor and the Ministers, who were supported by the State Council, a serious attempt was made to work a most difficult Constitution, and there was no non-cooperation.

The Constitution of 1931 had been accepted by the unofficial members of the Legislative Council by a majority of two only. As soon as it came into operation efforts were made both by the State Council and by the Board of Ministers to persuade the Government of the United Kingdom to accept amendments in the direction of self-government. These efforts failed until 1943, when the train of events leading to Dominion Status in 1948 was set in motion. Though the State Council was virtually agreed on the need for self-government, it was not agreed on its form. Communal representation having been abolished in 1931, the island was divided into fifty territorial constituencies, approximately equal in size. If the electorate wished to vote communally, and apparently it did, it was possible for the Sinhalese to win every constituency save four in the Northern Province, which would be won by Ceylon Tamils, and two in the Eastern Province, both of which would probably be won by Ceylon Tamils also. Thus the Sinhalese, who were 66 per cent. of the population, could obtain 88 per cent. of the territorial constituencies; the Ceylon Tamils, who were 11 per cent. of the population, could obtain 12 per cent. of those constituencies; and the Indians, Muslims, Burghers, and Europeans could obtain no constituencies at all.

The Ceylon Tamils, who had been over-represented proportionately under the Constitution of 1924, had voted solidly against the Constitution of 1931 and in the Jaffna Peninsula the elections of that year were boycotted. Three Tamils were, however, elected for other constituencies, a Muslim was returned for a seat in the Eastern Province, and two Europeans were elected for what might have been Sinhalese seats. For the rest, the minorities had to rely on eight seats filled by the Governor. In 1931 he appointed two Indians, a Muslim, a Burgher, and four Europeans. The representation varied somewhat as a result of by-elections and the general election of 1935–6, but the strength of the Sinhalese in the country was over-represented in the State Council. In 1931 a Muslim, an Indian, and five Sinhalese were elected as Ministers; but since the Muslim and the Indian dissented from the constitutional proposals of their colleagues, it was arranged in 1936 that there should be a Sinhalese majority on each executive committee and that each committee should elect a Sinhalese. A so-called Pan-Sinhalese Ministry thus came into being and the minorities were excluded from office until 1942, when on the resignation of Sir Baron Jayatilaka a Ceylon Tamil was elected Minister for Home Affairs. Of the seven Ministers elected in 1936 four were still in office in 1947. No parties had developed, and indeed it was virtually impracticable to operate a party system so long as the executive committees remained in being.

The undertaking given in 1943 was the result of much debate and correspondence. Its immediate cause, however, was the Cripps offer to India. The Ceylonese politicians felt aggrieved that an offer of Dominion Status has been made in India, where the Constitution of 1935 had virtually broken down and the politicians were in opposition, whereas in Ceylon the Constitution of 1931 was in full operation and the

Ministers and the State Council were collaborating in the war effort. It is believed that Admiral Sir Geoffrey Layton, who had assumed office as Commander-in-Chief after the fall of Singapore, urged that some action should be taken in order that the collaboration might be maintained without a conflict over constitutional reform.

The undertaking was, however, a promise not of Dominion Status but of full internal self-government subject to conditions relating to external affairs and defence. The necessary steps would be taken at the end of the war, but meanwhile the Ministers were authorized to draft constitutional proposals, acceptance of which would be conditional on six conditions being satisfied and on the approval of three-quarters of all the members of the State Council excluding the Speaker. The Ministers drafted proposals accordingly and submitted them in February 1944; but in July 1944 it was announced that a Commission would be sent to Ceylon to examine these proposals and the position generally. Believing this decision to be contrary to the undertaking of May 1943 the Ministers and most of the majority group in the State Council refrained from giving evidence, but there was no boycott of the Commission, which in September 1945 supported the Ministers' scheme with the addition of a Second Chamber and minor amendments. Meanwhile, Mr. D. S. Senanayake, Leader of the State Council, had been invited to London and had made a plea for Dominion Status. This was rejected, but in a White Paper of October 1945 substantial modifications of the limitations on self-government were made, and the scheme as amended was accepted by the State Council by 51 votes to 3, only the two Indian members (who wanted a change in the franchise to admit all Indians of five years' residence) and one Sinhalese communist voting against. The steps necessary to bring the new Constitution, that of 1946, into operation were then taken, and in February 1947 Mr. D. S. Senanayake renewed his plea for Dominion Status. In June 1947 this request was granted and tentative agreements were made for submission to the Ceylon Cabinet after the general election. The Cabinet agreeing in November, the agreements were signed, the Ceylon Independence Act, 1947, was passed, and the provisions of the Constitution inconsistent with Dominion Status were removed. Thus, when the island became a Dominion on 4 February 1948, it had a complete Constitution. India and Pakistan had become Dominions on 15 August· 1947, but temporarily they were governed under the Government of India Act, 1935, as amended, pending the drafting of new Constitutions.

In spite of the subsequent changes, the Constitution of 1947 is fundamentally the Ministers' scheme of 1944 with a weak Senate added and the restrictions on self-government deleted. It is short and therefore elastic, containing only eighty clauses and occupying only twenty-six printed pages. This simplicity was the result of deliberate policy. The Ministers' primary aim in 1944 was to secure as large a measure of self-government as possible and at the same time to provide a Constitution sufficiently flexible to enable it to be adapted to the difficult social and economic conditions of the island. It was desired, too, to abolish the fragmentation of policy inherent in the Constitution of 1931 and to vest power emphatically in a Cabinet responsible to the Legislature. Finally, the Ministers assumed that they would have to secure for their scheme a three-quarters majority in the State Council and that the less there was in the Constitution the fewer would be the items of controversy.

These aims were not always compatible. For instance, it was not enough to provide for a Cabinet and to assume the development of suitable constitutional conventions as had been done in the other Dominions. In order to make certain that the Governor acted as constitutional monarch in all cases where he had not, under the undertaking of 1943, special powers, it was necessary formally to enact the British constitutional conventions. Moreover, neither the Ministers nor the State Council were accustomed to collective responsibility, and it was necessary to make the obligation not merely conventional but also legal, if only to show the required majority in the State Council that a large slice of self-government was being conferred. These precautions became unnecessary on the assumption of Dominion Status, but they continue to find a place in the Constitution of 1947.

The most difficult problem, however, was to solve the communal conflict, or at least to get so near a solution that a three-quarters majority of the State Council could be secured. For the latter purpose it was necessary to obtain forty-three votes. If the Sinhalese were unanimous, which seemed unlikely, the Ministers would still obtain only thirty-nine votes unless they could secure the support of some minority members. Moreover it was recognized that the new Constitution would not work if any important minority felt itself genuinely aggrieved.

There was, however, a fundamental divergence between the Ministers and some of the minorities. Emphasizing the need for the disappearance of communalism, the Ministers wanted territorial constituencies without reservation of seats for minorities, though they were equally anxious that so long as communal ideas prevailed all communities should be represented. In the course of the discussions of the past dozen years, however, certain of the minority leaders, especially the Ceylon Tamils, had worked out a theory of 'balanced representation' under which, by means of communal electorates or reservation of seats, the Sinhalese and the minorities would be equally balanced both in the Legislature and in the Executive. Even if this were a practicable scheme, it could not be accepted by the Ministers. On the other hand, it was impossible not to recognize that most of the communal groups wanted to be represented by members of those groups. The Ministers did not want Tamils, Muslims, and Indians to be elected as such, but they recognized the need for sufficient numbers of Tamils, Muslims, and Indians to be elected. They were prepared for any compromise which gave the minorities adequate, or more than adequate, representation, provided that they were elected as representatives of the people and not as communal representatives.

This may seem a fine distinction, but it is recognized elsewhere. Nearly all the members of the House of Commons elected for Scottish constituencies are Scotsmen; they are, however, elected not as Scotsmen but as Conservative or Labour supporters. Scotsmen would be annoyed, and might develop a Scottish separationist movement, if there were not enough Scotsmen in the House; but Scots fight Scots on issues which are not Scottish but British. Similarly, the Ministers wanted a sufficiency of Tamils in the Legislature, but they wanted Tamils to fight Tamils on issues which might be described as Ceylonese. The difference between the United Kingdom and Ceylon is that though there are in the United Kingdom areas which are specifically English, Scottish, Welsh, and Northern Irish, Ceylon cannot easily be divided into Sinhalese, Tamil, Muslim, and Indian areas. One can secure an adequate number of Scotsmen by giving Scotland adequate representation. There is no Tamil, Indian, or Muslim equivalent of Scotland.

The solution to this problem was obviously to give weightage to those Provinces in which the minorities predominated: but how were those Provinces to be defined? There was much discussion over numbers, though it never came down to precise details. There was general agreement that there should be one hundred members, but the number of Sinhalese members suggested varied from sixty-five to fifty. Obviously a controversy of this kind could not be based on a principle, and therefore no agreement could be reached. Nor was it easy to see how the minority seats could be divided among the several communities. Finally, the Kandyans would want weightage against the low-country Sinhalese; and, if this was done, how was it possible to distinguish between Indian seats and Kandyan seats in the Kandyan Provinces, where the valleys are populated by Kandyans and the intervening ridges by Indians?

In short, this system had most of the disadvantages of communal representation. The only substantial difference would be that the electorates were not specifically communal and in most cases would be mixed. Clearly it was necessary to find some principle by means of which the Provinces containing minorities in strength could be given extra votes. The Provinces in which the communities would be strongest were as follows:

Low-country Sinhalese: Western, Southern, and North-Western Provinces.

Kandyan Sinhalese: Central, North-Central, and North-Western Provinces and Provinces of Uva and Sabaragamuwa.

Indians: Central Province and Provinces of Uva and Sabaragamuwa.

Muslims: Eastern and Northern Provinces.

Tamils: Northern and Eastern Provinces.

This distribution in itself gives a hint of the solution. The western and southern Provinces are densely populated. If seats are given for area as well for population the low-country Sinhalese will proportionately be reduced. Experiment showed that if on the 1931 population figures one seat were given for 75,000 population and one seat for 1,000 square miles of area, the distribution would be as follows:[1]

Province	Population	Area	Total
Western . . .	19	1	20
Southern . . .	10	2	12
North-Western . .	7	3	10
Central . . .	13	2	15
North-Central . .	1	4	5
Uva	4	3	7
Sabaragamuwa . .	8	2	10
Eastern . . .	3	4	7
Northern . . .	5	4	9
	70	25	95

[1] Sessional Paper XIV of 1944, p. 4.

Thus, the Provinces in which the communities were specially interested would have weightage for area as follows:

Community	Population	Area	Percentage weightage
Low-Country Sinhalese . .	36	6	14·3
Kandyan Sinhalese . . .	33	14	29·9
Indians	25	7	21·9
Muslims	8	8	50·0
Tamils	8	8	50·0

This scheme was approved by the Ministers. It was also agreed that the constituencies should be delimited by a Delimitation Commission, which should provide that each electoral district in a Province should have as nearly as might be an equal number of inhabitants, but should also take into account the transport facilities of the Province, its physical features, and 'the community or diversity of its inhabitants'. The Soulbury Commission approved the scheme but modified the language of the instructions to the Delimitation Commission so as to give more emphasis to the power to take 'community or diversity of interest' into account and less emphasis to the factor of equality. The Commission also suggested that the Delimitation Commision should have power to provide multi-member constituencies, especially to meet the caste problem. This would not in itself assist minority representation, but the Board of Ministers agreed to the 'plumping' of votes in multi-member constituencies; that is, in a three-member constituency each elector should be given three votes to cast as he pleased. It was assumed that the minorities—whether defined by race, caste, or religion—would tend to 'plump' their votes on minority candidates, while the majority community would tend to distribute one vote to each of three candidates.

The Ministers' scheme was unlikely to give adequate representation to the Burghers and Europeans, who played a large part in the economic life of the country. Since only about half the adult Indians had the franchise and the Indian areas were separated from each other by densely populated Kandyan village-areas, it was also possible that the Indians would be under-represented. The Ministers therefore authorized the Governor in his discretion to nominate six members. This discretionary power of the Governor became in 1948 an ordinary function of the Governor-General, to be exercised on ministerial advice.

The Ministers had decided not to suggest a Second Chamber. They were not agreed on the need and they were quite certain that they could not formulate a scheme which would secure a three-quarters majority in the State Council. Accordingly, they left the question to be settled by simple majority in the new Parliament. The Soulbury Commission, however, recommended a Senate on the Burma model. Fifteen senators were to be elected by the House of Representatives by means of the single transferable vote, while fifteen were to be nominated by the Governor in his discretion. A senator was to hold office for nine years, one-third of the senators retiring every three years. On Mr. Senanayake's representation, however, the period was reduced to six years, one-third of the senators retiring every two years. Also, though the first batch of senators was appointed by the Governor in his discretion, the changes of 1948 assumed that in future the Governor-General would act on 'advice'.

The powers of the Senate were, however, rigidly limited. In effect, it can like the House of Lords delay a 'money Bill' for one month; but the experience of the Parliament Act in the United Kingdom enabled a broader definition of 'money Bill' to be drafted. Any other Bill can be delayed for a period which need not exceed six months. The Senate is thus the least potent of the Second Chambers in the Commonwealth. Nor does its composition add to its power. The nominated members are notable more for their influence in the economic life of the country than for their efficiency as politicians, and in fact, now that the power of appointment is virtually in the hands of the Prime Minister, it is possible for them to be

Government 'yes-men'. Nor were active politicians elected by the House of Representatives. The Senate's detachment from party politics may yet make it a sobering influence when excitement reigns in the House of Representatives, but in present conditions, with a right-centre Government in power, its main function is to cross the *t*s and dot the *i*s of the debates in the other House.

The legislative powers of Parliament were limited in one respect only. In order to demonstrate their goodwill to the minorities and to obtain their support when the Ministers' scheme was submitted to them, the Sinhalese Ministers imposed a limitation on communal legislation. No law may—

(*a*) prohibit or restrict the free exercise of any religion; or

(*b*) make persons of any community or religion liable to disabilities or restrictions to which persons of other communities or religions are not made liable; or

(*c*) confer on persons of any community or religion any privilege or advantage which is not conferred on persons of other communities or religions; or

(*d*) alter the constitution of any religious body except with the consent of the governing authority of that body.

In the process of drafting, this last restriction was strengthened by adding that where a religious body was incorporated by law (e.g. the Roman Catholic Church), no such alteration should be made except at the request of its governing authority.

Finally, another provision was inserted to meet the fears of the minorities. The Ceylon Tamils are over-represented in the public service because of the eagerness with which they have made use of English education. It was thought by the Ministers that the fear of the loss of this advantage, and even of the substitution of under-representation for over-representation, was one cause of the Tamil demand for 'balanced representation'. It was therefore decided to establish an independent Public Service Commission empowered to make all appointments to the public service above a low salary level. The Soulbury Commission went farther and recommended the vesting in the Public Service Commission of power over the appointment, dismissal, transfer, and disciplinary control of public officers. This extension was accepted by Mr. D. S. Senanayake and incorporated into the Constitution.

It will be seen that every effort was made to provide a fair compromise of opposing theses. Such a compromise was necessary if the Ministers were to obtain the support of three-quarters of the Council; but this tactical objective must not hide the strategy. The desire to take communalism out of politics was expressed by Mr. Senanayake not only while the need for the large majority existed but also after the requirement was withdrawn in October 1945. Independently of the requirement of the majority, he desired a demonstration of unanimity in order that his case for Dominion Status might be strengthened. Even this is not a full explanation; for after the huge majority of fifty-one votes to three had been obtained and a promise of Dominion Status secured, no attempt was made to whittle down the protection to minorities. Mr. Senanayake formed the United National Party before the general election of 1947, and formed his Government after the general election, on a non-communal basis. Clearly, the fundamental desire was not to secure tactical advantages but to leave the racial and religious communities as purely cultural bodies outside the political orbit.

VII

THE CONSTITUTION OF INDIA

AS in Ceylon, the 'representative' element in Indian government was introduced by way of nomination. An elective element was first introduced into local government and was not extended to the Government of India until the Morley–Minto reform of 1909. Nominations were inevitably on communal lines, using that term in its widest sense so as to include economic as well as racial, religious, and caste groups. Though much larger in scale and much more complex, the problem was the same in India as in Ceylon, namely, that the nominated Indians could not be said to be representative unless they were selected from each of the major social groups. The foundation of communal representation was thus communal nomination, and communal nomination was the only means by which Indians could be associated with the Government. It was of no great importance so long as there was everywhere an official majority, as there was until 1909, but its character changed as soon as Indians formed a majority, for then it became a contest for power. Communal representation did not create communalism; it provided the means for communalism to organize itself more highly.

As in Ceylon, too, the demand for representation was associated with a demand for jobs. The Indian National Congress, which was founded in 1885, was in its origin a middle-class body and remained dominated by middle-class elements. It had at first two aims, to increase the Indian element in the services and to increase the representative element in the legislatures. Even at this early stage there were Muslims who saw dangers in the increasing economic and political status of the Hindus and followed the advice of Sir Sanyed Ahmad Khan to avoid membership of the Congress;

and though it always had members from other communities the Congress was primarily Hindu.

The Morley–Minto reform of 1909 broadened the membership of the legislatures and accepted the principle of election, but continued the old principle of the representation of special interests, including the Muslims. The reforms of 1919 and 1935 broadened the sphere of self-government but continued the same essential principle of the representation of interests. Even so the Muslim League became more and more intransigent while the Congress, feeling itself more and more frustrated, became increasingly revolutionary. After several efforts at a settlement by agreement in 1940, 1942, and 1946, the British Government at last cut the Gordian knot in 1947, announced its determination to quit India, and virtually left the Congress with the choice between splitting India through the creation of Pakistan and starting a civil war in order to maintain its unity. The Congress leadership, which had already missed opportunities in 1940 and 1942 of retaining the unity of India by some form of devolution, rightly chose the peaceful alternative.

A Constituent Assembly had been set up for undivided India in 1946 and after partition it became the Constituent Assembly for the Dominion of India. It also functioned as the federal legislature under the Government of India Act, 1935, which was modified by temporary legislation to suit the new conditions. Though the Congress, which had become dominant through the independence of India and the separation of Pakistan, had from the beginning repudiated the Act of 1935, it was the Constitution in being and some of its characteristics were inevitably translated into the 1950 Constitution.

It was in the first place a federal Constitution. Undivided India was too vast a country to be governed democratically as a unit. It is significant that even in the Union of India under the 1950 Constitution every member of the House of the People has to represent between 500,000 and 750,000 people. It was, too, so diverse a country that some degree of local autonomy had to be established. The Sikhs of the Punjab may be happy to be fellow citizens with the Tamils of Madras, but they are so different in religion, language, social conditions, food, clothing, and even physique that a differentiation must be drawn in matters of government also. Even after separation, the new Constitution schedules thirteen languages (as well as Sanskrit), and these are not dialects—of which there are several hundred—but fundamentally different languages.

There was, too, the problem of the Indian States. It was, indeed, the prospect that most of them would accede to the federation that induced the National (or Conservative) Government of 1934–5 to contemplate a substantial measure of self-government at the centre as well as internal self-government in the provinces of British India. When they failed to accede the federal provisions of the 1935 Act were not put into operation. Nor was there a similar complication in 1950, for the Congress Government had been able to bring pressure to bear on the princes, and by 1950 the smaller States had been absorbed into provinces or into groups of States; and the larger States could be treated, with minor modifications, like the Provinces.

The enormous complication of the Government of India Act was also due to the numerous 'safeguards' put in for the protection of minorities and the provision made for communal electorates, reserved seats, and nominated seats in order to secure adequate representation for the numerous communal groups of undivided India. These, too, virtually disappeared in 1950. The 'surgical' operation which created Pakistan removed the major communal problem of undivided India, and for the rest the Congress theory that the communal problem could be solved by a federation and a Bill of Rights was put into the new Constitution.

Finally, the Government of India Act included much detail about judicial and administrative arrangements which is normally left to ordinary legislation. Powers for this purpose had formerly been exercised by the Viceroy and the Governors of Provinces and had to be distributed among the new authorities. In 1950 they had to be redistributed. This could easily have been done by authorizing the Union Parliament to enact the ·necessary legislation; but the precedent having been set in 1935 was followed in 1950. In relation to these matters the Constitution seems to be unnecessarily complicated.

All this helps to explain why the Constitution is one of the longest ever devised for an independent country. It comprises 395 sections and seven schedules, occupying altogether 250 pages. The explanation is not, however, complete. In the first place, the Constituent Assembly contained a high proportion of lawyers accustomed to the complications of modern legislation and the extreme formality of the administrative process in British India. They had no experience of simpler Constitutions but were familiar with the complexity of the Act of 1935. Inevitably they sought certainty in careful drafting and were not impressed with the need for flexibility in a Constitution which may determine the destinies of India for centuries. In the second place, the Constituent Assembly was a large body representing all the diversities of one of the world's most heterogeneous populations. The fact that a reasonably agreed draft could be produced in one year and a complete Constitution in little more than two years bears witness to the admirable spirit in which the discussions were conducted; but there were many diverse points of view to be met and many opinions to be placated, with the result that a complicated series of compromises—noticeable especially in the relations between the Union and the States—had to be drafted.

The complications of the Government of India Act were not important because if they gave rise to difficulties an amending Act could easily and quickly be passed by the Parliament of the United Kingdom. It was indeed an experimental and transitional Constitution intended to lead in due course to a self-governing India. The Constitution of India, on the other hand, provides a permanent system of government. Containing many provisions inserted in order to effect compromises among competing interests, it had to be made somewhat rigid. An ordinary amendment requires an absolute majority of all the members in each House of Parliament and a two-thirds majority of those present and voting in each House. The House of the People represents the electors in proportion to population. The Council of States, the second chamber, represents the States according to a fixed schedule, in the case of a Class A or Class B State[1] the representatives being elected by the elected members of the Legislative Assembly by means of the single transferable vote. To secure a two-thirds majority in each House for any controversial amendment will therefore be a difficult task. Even so, there are over sixty sections, including the very complicated judicial clauses and most of the clauses governing the relations between the Union and the States, and also the Seventh Schedule, which distributes legislative powers, which can be amended by this procedure only if an affirmative resolution is passed in the legislatures of half the Class A and Class B States. This does not add very much to the requirements, for if more than half the States are against the amendment it is reasonably certain that the Council of States will be against it. Nevertheless, the Constitution is at once very detailed and very rigid, a combination of qualities which may well give rise to difficulties. It is a useful rule not to put into a Constitution anything which can safely be left to ordinary legislation; but if for any reason it is necessary to make the Constitution detailed it is also necessary to make as much as possible amendable by the simplest possible procedure. The Constituent Assembly has not followed this rule, but has prescribed its own solution to most of the current difficulties and made it difficult for future generations to adopt a different solution.

[1] i.e. a former Governor's Province or a former Indian State or a combination of Indian States.

Fortunately, the State system has been very much simplified through the reorganization of the Indian States effected by the provisional Government of India, under authority conferred by the Constituent Assembly as legislature, after the disappearance of the paramountcy of the Crown. Of the twelve Provinces of British India three—Sind, North-West Frontier Province, and Baluchistan—went to Pakistan; two —Bengal and the Punjab—were divided; and the remaining seven went to the Dominion of India. The Union of India therefore contains nine of these States, including West Bengal and Punjab (formerly East Punjab). These are scheduled in Part A of the First Schedule and may be described as Class A States. The remainder of the Dominion of India consisted of a multitude of States under princely rule, whose number has been drastically reduced partly by incorporating small States in the neighbouring Provinces and partly by creating unions of States. Nine of the units so formed are large enough to form States of an Indian federation, with Constitutions similar in principle to those of the former Governors' Provinces or the present Class A States. They are listed in Part B of the First Schedule and may be called Class B States. They are Hyderabad, Jammu and Kashmir (for which special provision of a temporary character has been made in view of the current controversy with Pakistan), Madhya Bharat (a union of Malwa States including Gwalior), Mysore, Patiala and East Punjab States, Rajasthan (a union of Rajput States), Saurashtra (a union of States in the former Bombay Presidency), Travancore-Cochin, and Vindhya Pradesh (a union of States in the former Central Provinces).

Apart from the Andaman and Nicobar Islands, there remain only ten areas outside the Class A and Class B States, and they are listed in Part C of the First Schedule. These Class C States are administered by the President through a Chief Commissioner, a Lieutenant-Governor, or the Governor or Rajpramukh of a neighbouring State. If separately administered a Class C State may be provided with a legislature and a Council of Advisers or Ministers. Of these ten Class C States, three were formerly Chief Commissioners' Provinces —Ajmer, Coorg, and Delhi; six were princely States— Bhopal, Bilaspur, Cooch Behar, Kutch, Manipur, and Tripura; and the last is Himachal Pradesh, a union of States.

The Class B States are to be governed in the same way as Class A States, the only essential difference being that the Governor is replaced by the Maharajah or (in a union of States) one of the Maharajahs as Rajpramukh. Each will have an elected legislature (with two Houses in Mysore) and a Council of Ministers. No doubt some time will elapse before the extremely sensitive and jealous Rajput States, for instance, get used to a joint democratic Constitution, but this is the sort of difficulty that time will remove. An immense simplification of an extraordinarily complex organization has been effected by the Constituent Assembly.

It may be noted that no attempt has been made to alter the boundaries established by the British administration. Those boundaries had little relation to geographical and ethnic conditions because they depended upon successive extensions of British control from the three main settlements or 'presidencies' in Bombay, Madras, and Calcutta. Even some of the States—for instance Hyderabad—were artificial creations from British rule, and generally the existence of a State depended on the loyalty of the ruler—which often depended on the amount of his subsidy—to the British authority in India. South India, for instance, is divided into one Class A State—Madras—and the Class B States of Hyderabad, Mysore, and Travancore-Cochin. The linguistic areas are quite different and, if boundaries were drawn on the basis of language, would require the redivision of the whole area according to the distribution of Tamil, Telugu, Malayalam, and Kannada. The Telugus have been the most insistent, and there is some prospect of an Andhra State being carved out of Madras and Orissa. Generally, however, the Government of India, supported by the Constituent Assembly, has damped down the enthusiasm for linguistic States. Local or provincial nationalism used to be an ally in the fight against British rule; now it is an enemy of Indian nationalism. Nor is it wholly altruistic, for behind it is the most difficult problem that the ordinary Indian parent has to face: how to get his son into a lucrative and comfortable government job. If—to take that example, which does not stand alone—there is an Andhra State its language of administration will be Telugu and the government service will be staffed by Telugus instead of by Tamils, whose appreciation of English education, or at least of its benefits, and whose capacity for sustained hard work have given them a considerable advantage.

THE LANGUAGE PROBLEM

This, of course, raises the whole language issue. The nationalist politician was English-speaking and his nationalism was derived from the reading of English history; but his antagonism to British rule and his sympathy with the Indian masses who knew no English made him an opponent of the English language. On the other hand, it was English which unified India and, now that British rule has disappeared, its value to Indian nationalism has become apparent. The most widely-spoken Indian language is Hindi, but it has several varieties and is the language of the Ganges Valley. Though the nationalists of the other parts of India would wish, as a matter of self-respect, to substitute an Indian language for English, they do not like to contemplate the transitional period, in which those who speak Hindi as well as English will have an advantage over those who speak Assamese or Bengali, Gujarati or Marathi, Punjabi or Kashmiri, Tamil, Telugu, Malayalam, or Kannada, or Oriya. Nor is Hindi as yet adapted to becoming the language of the courts or of administration.

These considerations have suggested the curious compromise of Part XVII of the Constitution, where nine sections, occupying five pages, are required to regulate what is described as 'official language'—in the singular. That official language is to be Hindi in Devanagari script. For fifteen years, however, 'the English language shall continue to be used for all the official purposes of the Union for which it was used immediately before' 26 January 1950. This is qualified by the power of the President to authorize the use of Hindi in addition to English for any of the official purposes of the Union. This would be clear enough if it stood alone: English would be used until 1965, subject to the power of the President to authorize the use of Hindi also; after 1965 Hindi would be used. Lest this be optimistic, however, another clause has been inserted empowering the President, after 1965, to authorize the use of English for such purposes as may be specified by law.

Meanwhile, in 1955 and again in 1960, the President must appoint a Commission consisting of a Chairman and members representing the fourteen scheduled languages of India (including Sanskrit, which nobody speaks as a living language, but which some would like to see converted into the national language). Its function will be to advise the President on the progressive use of Hindi, restrictions on the use of English, the legal language of India, the form of numerals, and other linguistic matters. In making recommendations the Commission 'shall have due regard to the industrial, cultural, and scientific advancement of India, and the just claims and the interests of persons belonging to the non-Hindi-speaking areas in regard to the public services'. This precautionary drafting indicates the case against Hindi: that until it is sufficiently developed its use will obstruct the intellectual development of India, and that its use favours the Hindi-speaking section of the population.

It is further provided that the recommendations of the Commission will be considered by what is in fact a joint select committee of both Houses, consisting of twenty members elected by the House of the People and ten members elected by the House of the States, in each case by single transferable vote. After consideration of the Committee's report on the Council's recommendations, the President 'may issue directions in accordance with the whole or any part of that report'.

The State legislatures are empowered to adopt for official purposes any of the languages used in the State, or Hindi; but until a State does, English will be used. What is more, in order to prevent communal discrimination the President of the Union is authorized to direct that a language spoken by a substantial proportion of the population shall also be used.

All this does not apply to the Supreme Court and the High Courts of the States, to Bills in the legislatures, Acts and Ordinances enacted, and statutory instruments. Until the Parliament of the Union otherwise provides, these must be in English. The Governor or Rajpramukh of a State may, with the previous consent of the President, authorize the use of Hindi or any other official language in the High Court, though judgements, decrees, and orders must be in English. Also, the State legislature may authorize the use of some language other than English for Bills, Acts, and delegated legislation: but a translation in English must be published and the English text will be authoritative. All this is, of course, until Parliament otherwise provides: but a Bill or motion may not be introduced into Parliament without the President's consent, and he may not consent until he has taken into consideration the recommendations of the Commission and the report of the committee mentioned above.

These complicated and tortuous provisions bear witness to the difficulty of the problem, but they also bear witness to the realism with which the problem has been approached. Even if Hindi had been sufficiently developed to make it suitable for legal administration and higher education it would not be easy to substitute it for a language which has been a *lingua franca* for educated Indians for a century. In fact, however, it is not: and even fifteen years—which is a much longer period than was contemplated two years ago—may be too short a period. It may indeed be doubted whether the effort is worth while. Every educated Indian will have to learn to read English even when Hindi becomes the language of the Union. He will, presumably, be educated in his State language, or one of them; unless that language is Hindi he will have to become fluent in Hindi if he wishes to join a profession or secure employment outside his own State or even to secure higher employment in his own State; and he will need to learn English to make the professional literature of the world available to him. The task is not impossible, but it seems clear that for a substantial period at least the Indian contribution to literature, science, and technology will be small.

THE MACHINERY OF GOVERNMENT

Strange though it may seem, the machinery of government provided for the Union and the States is fundamentally British. Though India has become a 'sovereign democratic republic' and will have an elected President, he will in fact be a constitutional monarch. The Constitution has been framed by lawyers accustomed to the legal concept of 'the Crown' and the conventional system of Cabinet government. Though neither the Crown nor Cabinet government appears in the Constitution as such, they are in fact there. The drafting would have been simpler and the Constitution would have worked in almost precisely the same way if there had been a Governor-General appointed by the King and Governors appointed by the Governor-General. The repudiation of the formal link with the Crown was, however, a declaration of independence, an emotional luxury which the Congress thought it owed to itself in view of the grievances which many of its members had accumulated against 'the Crown' when it was represented by the Viceroy of India.

The President is elected by an electoral college consisting of the elected members of both Houses of Parliament and the elected members of the legislative assemblies of the States, the votes being weighted to secure representation according to population. He is 'aided and advised' by a Council of

Ministers which is collectively responsible to the House of the People and which is a Cabinet under a more appropriate name. In a Class A State the Governor is appointed by the President during pleasure; and he too is 'aided and advised' by a Council of Ministers which is collectively responsible to the legislative assembly. There are, however, a few functions which he exercises 'in his discretion' and not on the advice of Ministers. The Rajpramukh of a Class B State is in Hyderabad the Nizam, in Kashmir and Mysore the Maharajah, and elsewhere the person (usually one of the rulers) recognized by the President as Rajpramukh. He also is 'aided and advised' by a Council of Ministers collectively responsible to the legislative assembly.

The very diversity of India may enable the Cabinet system to work smoothly in the Union. In a country with only two 'communities', like the English and the Scots, it would be difficult for the Cabinet system to function if voting were on communal lines. If the English formed a Cabinet the Scots would be an irresponsible Opposition because they would never get a majority and be compelled to carry out their promises and to give effect to their criticisms. If, on the other hand, the English and the Scots formed a coalition, collective responsibility would be something of a fiction, for the English would be responsible to the English and the Scots to the Scots. The system would work, as indeed it does in the House of Commons, if the House divided not according to 'community' but according to parties and policies.

India will take some time to develop a party system, though it is developing through the growth of opposition to the Congress. But there is much less fear of communalism in the Union than in the States. In the Union the number of 'communities' is large, none having a majority. The Council of Ministers is and must be a coalition in communal terms; but it is so much a coalition that the communal terms are quite irrelevant. There may be a fear at a later stage of a division between the Hindi-speaking and the non-Hindi-speaking sections, for the language will then create an artificial barrier, but at the moment there can be no communal division because there are too many communities. This would not have been so if the Muslim provinces had remained within the Union, for then there would have been a fundamental division between Hindu and Muslim.

Fear of communalism arises not in the Union but in the States. Kashmir with its Muslim majority and Hindu dominant class, and Hyderabad with its Hindu majority governed until recently by a Muslim minority, are obvious examples; but there are sources of dissension even in an area so remote from the Hindu-Muslim conflict as Madras, where the conflict between Brahmans and non-Brahmans is by no means settled. It is a relevant factor that, apart from the Bill of Rights, the Constitution virtually ignores the communal problem. Reservation of seats for the scheduled castes and scheduled tribes is provided in the House of the People. The President is empowered to appoint two Anglo-Indians to the House of the People. Seats in the legislative assemblies of the States are to be reserved for members of the scheduled castes and the scheduled tribes, and the Governor or Rajpramukh may nominate Anglo-Indians. But these provisions will all disappear in 1960. For ten years, too, the Anglo-Indians are to be protected in respect of appointments to certain branches of the public service: but this protection will progressively disappear.

The only other form of protection arises from the establishment of a Public Service Commission for the Union and a Public Service Commission for each State. The members will be appointed by the President, the Governor, or the Rajpramukh, as the case may be; and one-half of the members must have been officials. The Commissions are independent bodies, but their functions are much more limited than in Ceylon, where the full power of appointment, transfer, dismissal, and disciplinary control is vested in the Commission. Apart from the holding of examinations, their function is to give advice to the Government of India or the Government of the State. The Constitution therefore gives no protection against communalism, corruption, or favouritism in the making of appointments and transfers in the public service.

These provisions, or the lack of provisions, for protection against discrimination suggest a considerable degree of optimism in the Constituent Assembly which Indian conditions do not warrant. As was mentioned in an earlier chapter of this book, it was a Congress thesis that communalism was a product of, or was exacerbated by, British rule; and the Constituent Assembly has decided to put this theory to the test.

Apart from the temporary provision for reserved seats and nominated members, the sections of the Constitution relating to the legislatures ignore the communal problem. There is not even the concession of weightage given in Ceylon. The Union Parliament consists of two Houses, the House of the People and the Council of States. The House of the People is to consist of not more than 500 members directly elected by the people of the States on the basis of one member for every 500,000 to 750,000 population. The right to vote is given to every citizen of India who is not less than 21 years of age on the qualifying date and is not disqualified. Subject to these rules the distribution of seats, the delimitation of constituencies, and election law generally are left to be governed by ordinary legislation. Provision is made for an Election Commission, consisting of a Chief Election Commissioner and other Commissioners appointed by the President. The Chief Election Commissioner may not be removed from office except in the same manner and on like grounds as a judge of the Supreme Court, while any other Commissioner may not be removed from office except on the recommendation of the Chief Election Commissioner. The Commission is charged with the superintendence, direction, and control of the preparation of the electoral rolls for, and the conduct of, all elections to Parliament and to State legislatures and of elections to the offices of President and Vice-President.

It will be seen, however, that the really contentious questions, the determination of the size of constituencies (which may vary from 500,000 to 750,000 population) and the delimitation of boundaries of constituencies, are given no constitutional protection whatever. These questions are more contentious in India than in many other countries because the various communities—linguistic, religious, and caste—are often in 'pockets'. If the pocket is large enough and is included in a single constituency, the community will dominate that constituency and return a member of its own kind: if the pocket is divided, the community may obtain no representation at all. A similar problem in Ceylon was met by establishing an independent Delimitation Commission and instructing it to pay attention to 'community or diversity of interest'. It may be intended to make similar provision by law in India, but such a law will carry no constitutional guarantee and will be under the control of a parliamentary majority in both Houses. What is more, after every census the constituencies 'shall be readjusted by such authority, in such manner and with effect from such date as Parliament may by law determine'. It is curious that a Constitution which goes into vast detail over comparatively unimportant institutions like the High Courts should be so vague and general on the extremely important subject of parliamentary representation. This seems to arise on the one hand because of the predominance of lawyers in the Constituent Assembly and on the other hand because of the Congress belief that the communal problem has been grossly exaggerated. There is no doubt that the problem has been exaggerated, but it still exists and indeed is implicit in the structure of Indian society.

The Council of States is to consist of twelve members nominated by the President because of their special knowledge or practical experience in such matters as literature, science, art, and social service, and of not more than 238 representatives of the States. The number of such representatives is apparently fixed for all time (subject to constitutional amendment) by the Fourth Schedule, which gives 145 seats to the Class A States, 53 seats to the Class B States, and seven to the Class C States. On the basis of the 1941 census, this gives one seat for a population varying from one million to two millions, though it is not easy to see the basis of the variation. Assam and Kashmir, for instance, seem to be over-represented while Madras is under-represented. There have, however, been so many changes of population due to the absorption of States and the influx of refugees that this may not be an accurate analysis.

The elected members of the Council of States for each State will be elected by the elected members of the legislative assembly of that State by means of the single transferable vote. Since the elected members of the legislative assembly will each represent a unit of about 75,000 population, the effect of the single transferable vote may be to give representation in the Council of States which is communally more diverse than that in the House of the People, where a unit of the order of 300,000 in a constituency varying from 500,000 to 750,000 will be necessary to secure representation. It is probable, too, that the system of indirect representation will give a greater emphasis to 'States' rights' than the system of direct election to the House of the People. In other words, the two Houses may well represent opposing points of view on current affairs. What is more, while the House of the People may be dissolved and is automatically dissolved at the end of five years, the Council of States is not subject to dissolution but one-third of the members retire in every second year. It follows that the latter will be less adaptable to changing opinion.

The relations between the Houses, as in the United Kingdom, depend upon whether the Bill under discussion is or is not a Money Bill. The definition is based on that in the Parliament Act, 1911, and seems to have much the same effect, though the drafting is different. The additions made in Ceylon to meet the difficulties experienced in the United

Kingdom have not been inserted: but these difficulties are not likely to be important in India, since the procedure for passing a Bill other than a Money Bill is comparatively simple.

A Money Bill must be introduced into the House of the People. After it has passed that House it must be transmitted to the Council of States, which must return it with its recommendations within fourteen days from its receipt. If any of the recommendations are accepted it is deemed to have been passed by both Houses with the amendments recommended and accepted. If none of the recommendations is accepted the Bill is deemed to have been passed by both Houses in the form in which it passed the House of the People. If it is not returned to the House of the People within fourteen days it is deemed to have been passed by both Houses in the form in which it passed the House of the People.

A Bill other than a Money Bill may originate in either House. If it has been passed by one House and transmitted to the other House and

(a) the Bill is rejected by the other House; or
(b) the Houses have finally disagreed as to the amendments to be made in the Bill; or
(c) more than six months elapse from the date of the reception of the Bill by the other House without its being passed by that House

the President may summon a joint sitting of both Houses. If it is then passed by a majority of the members sitting and voting, it is deemed to have passed both Houses.

The Constitution of India, unlike the Constitutions of most other federations, contains detailed provisions for the regulation of the States and, what is more, vests many of the constituent powers in the Parliament of the Union. Of the Class A States, Bihar, Bombay, Madras, Punjab, the United Provinces, and West Bengal will have two Houses, a Legislative Assembly and a Legislative Council. Assam, Madhya Pradesh, and Orissa will have unicameral legislatures. The distinction is based on population, except that Punjab is given a second chamber, perhaps because of the diversity of its population. Of the Class B States, only Mysore will have two Houses. The Union Parliament is, however, empowered to create or abolish a Legislative Council in any State if the Legislative Assembly passes a resolution to that effect by a majority of all its members and a two-thirds majority of those sitting and voting.

In each State the Legislative Assembly will consist of members elected for territorial constituencies, normally at the rate of one member for 75,000 population, though the number of members must not be less than 60 or more than 500. The Legislative Council must not have more than one-quarter of the number of members in the Legislative Assembly, with a minimum of 40 members. The Parliament of the Union is empowered to alter the composition of the Legislative Councils. Until it provides otherwise, e?ch Council will consist of:

(a) one-third elected by local authorities;

(b) one-twelfth elected by electorates composed of graduates of Indian universities or of persons having similar qualifications;

(c) one-twelfth of teachers in secondary schools or higher educational institutions;

(d) one-third elected by members of the Legislative Assembly from among persons who are not members of the Assembly;

(e) the remainder nominated by the Governor or the Rajpramukh from among persons who have special knowledge or practical experience in respect of such matters as literature, science, art, the co-operative movement, and social service.

The Legislative Assembly, like the House of the People, will last five years unless sooner dissolved by the Governor or Rajpramukh, while the Legislative Council, like the Council of

States, will not be subject to dissolution, but one-third of the members will retire in every second year. The relations between the two Houses are in substance the same as those between the House of the People and the Council of the States, with the qualification that the power of delaying a Bill is limited to three months and a joint sitting is not necessary. Also, whereas the President has power only to assent to a Bill, to refuse assent, or to refer it back for reconsideration, the Governor or Rajpramukh also has power to reserve a Bill for the President's assent and must do so if, in his opinion, the Bill would so derogate from the powers of the High Court as to endanger the position which it is designed by the Constitution to fill.

Following the precedent established by the Government of India Act, 1935, the division of powers between the Union and the States is set out in great detail. There are three long lists occupying fifteen printed pages. The Union list contains powers vested exclusively in the Union; the State list contains powers vested exclusively in the States; the concurrent list contains powers vested both in the Union and in the States. The residuary power is vested in the Union, so that if a power is not to be found in the State list or the concurrent list it must be vested exclusively in the Union. If a law made by a State legislature is repugnant to any provision of a law made by the Union Parliament which that Parliament is competent to enact, the State law is void; but if it comes within the concurrent list it will be valid if the Bill has been reserved for the President's consideration and has received his assent.

The subjects dealt with in the State list include police and public order, inferior courts, prisons, local government (including public health), intoxicating liquors, relief of the disabled and unemployable, education and libraries, local communications, agriculture, land and water, fisheries and forests, internal trade and gas supply, and markets and fairs. The concurrent list covers most branches of the civil and criminal law and civil and criminal procedure, food and drugs, economic and social planning, trade unions and trade disputes, the professions, factories and electricity. Other powers are in principle Union powers. The distribution was worked out carefully in the drafting of the Act of 1935. The changes in the new Constitution are few but significant. Into the concurrent list have been added 'economic and social planning', 'commercial and industrial monopolies, companies and trusts' and (in addition to 'social security and social insurance'), 'employment and unemployment'. These powers are of an order different from the order of the concurrent powers under the Act of 1935. They are broad and vague and not incidental to anything which appears in the Union list. They bear witness to the centralizing tendency of the Constituent Assembly.

One of the major difficulties of all federations is the distribution of financial resources. Again following the example of 1935 the Constituent Assembly has made a separate allocation of taxing power and has then, by financial clauses, redistributed the income thus made available. To the Union it has allocated taxes on income (other than agricultural income), customs duties, excise duties except on alcoholic liquor and narcotics, corporation taxes, capital taxes (except on agricultural land), estate and succession duties (except on agricultural land), taxes on fares and freights, and some of the stamp duties. To the States it has allocated taxes on agricultural income, estate and succession duty on agricultural land, taxes on lands and buildings, taxes on mineral rights, excise duties on alcoholic liquors and narcotics, taxes on the entry of consumption goods, sales taxes, capitation taxes, luxury taxes, and certain licence and stamp duties.

This distribution of taxing powers would not enable the States to carry out the important functions allocated to them, and accordingly a distribution of resources is effected. First, certain stamp duties and excise duties, though collected by the Union, will not pass into the Consolidated Fund of India but will be assigned to the States in which they were levied. Secondly, succession duties, estate duties, certain taxes on fares and freights, and a few others, are to be assigned to the States in accordance with a law passed by Parliament. Thirdly, income tax, subject to certain deductions, will be distributed according to a scheme formulated by the President on the recommendation of a Finance Commission. In all these cases, however, the Union Parliament may add a surcharge which will go to Union funds. Fourthly, excise duties other than those already mentioned may be transferred (via the Consolidated Fund) to the States by Act of Parliament. Fifthly, grants-in-aid must be paid to Assam, Bihar, Orissa, and West Bengal in lieu of assignment of the export duty on jute, though for a maximum period of ten years. Sixthly, power is given to Parliament to make grants-in-aid. Finally, provision is made for the establishment of a Finance Commission in or before 1952 and thereafter at intervals of five years, to make recommendations to the President about the distribution of financial resources and other specified financial questions.

THE BILL OF RIGHTS

It will be seen that the distribution of legislative powers is extremely complicated and that it must give rise to much litigation, though it is probable that drafting in detail has reduced the number of possible cases of conflict. To this it must be added that either Union or State legislation may be involved through infringement of the Bill of Rights contained in Part III of the Constitution. There are also in Part IV 'Directive Principles of State Policy', which are in fact a manifesto of political principles made sufficiently vague to secure wide acceptance. These directives are 'fundamental in the governance of the country and it shall be the duty of the State [which here includes the Union] to apply these principles in making laws'. They are not, however, enforceable in the courts.

The Bill of Rights refers to 'the State', which here includes the Union, the States in the narrower sense, and local authorities. Laws made by the State which infringe any of the fundamental rights are void.

The first group of rights are rights of equality, and it is in this group that the main remedy for communalism must be sought. Equality before the law is provided for and titles are forbidden, but the main provisions relate to social discrimination. 'Untouchability' is abolished and its practice in any form is forbidden. The enforcement of any disability arising out of 'untouchability' is to be an offence punishable in accordance with law. This is, of course, more easily said than done, and it is by no means clear what 'enforcement' means. If people leave a restaurant when an 'untouchable' enters or children are not sent to schools which accept 'untouchable' children, it would not be easy to say that 'untouchability' is being enforced. In this respect the Congress politicians are well ahead of public opinion. Having right and justice on their side they will, no doubt, win in the end, but in some parts of India this clause is likely to be a mere hypothesis for many years to come.

Further, the State is forbidden to discriminate against any citizen on grounds of religion, race, caste, sex, place of birth, or any of them. This is not in terms limited to law, but effective enforcement is difficult except in the case of law. Discrimination in respect of public employment is covered by another clause, but it is virtually impossible to prevent by law discrimination in respect of the location of schools, irrigation works, price controls, discretionary licences, and the rest. It must be remembered in particular that employment is still largely determined by caste, so that special legislation (e.g. through wages boards, licensing, &c.) applying to carpenters, fishermen, goldsmiths, toddy-tappers, and so on must inevitably apply to special castes. There need not be discrimination in fact: so long as the caste system prevails it will be alleged that there is discrimination.

The clause against discrimination, however, goes farther. It is provided that no citizen shall, on grounds only of religion, race, caste, sex, place of birth, or any of them, be subject to any disability, liability, restriction, or conditions with regard to—

(a) access to shops, public restaurants, hotels and places of public entertainment; or

(b) the use of wells, tanks, bathing ghats, roads and places of public resort maintained wholly or partly out of State funds or dedicated to the use of the general public.

One curious omission is that of cemeteries and crematoria, over which caste disputes frequently arise. In any case there is here no sanction except in the case of a public authority. What is more, the provision goes far beyond public opinion. Nothing in this clause stops, or can stop, a Brahman from refusing to eat in a non-Brahman restaurant, and if there is any real risk of a non-Brahman entering a Brahman restaurant many Brahmans will not use it. What is more, though a non-Brahman may enter a Brahman restaurant, there is no law to stop all the Brahmans from leaving it as soon as he does and staying away thereafter.

Equality of opportunity in employment in the public service is provided by a separate clause. No citizen may, on grounds only of religion, race, caste, sex, descent, place of birth, residence, or any of them, be ineligible for, or discriminated against in respect of, any employment or office under the State. There are, however, limitations. The Parliament of the Union (but not the legislature of a State) may make laws prescribing requirements as to residence for State employment. Also, 'the State' may reserve posts for members of 'any backward class of citizens which, in the opinion of the State, is not adequately represented in the services under the State'. Nor is there anything in the clause to prevent discrimination according to language. If, for instance, the

Madras Government required every officer to read and write Tamil the great mass of Indians, including many of those belonging to the State of Madras, would automatically be excluded. Nor in any case could a constitutional provision, however carefully drawn, prevent a selection board consisting of Hindus from preferring a Hindu candidate to an equally good Muslim candidate. After all, what is 'equally good' is often a mere matter of opinion.

Some of these exceptions, express and implied, may be cumulative. In most parts of India the caste Hindus will decide where schools are to be placed, and it would be surprising if they were all sufficiently enlightened to be willing to place schools where they are most needed, among the depressed classes; but if the depressed classes have no schools they cannot secure public employment or hope to have representatives in the legislatures. The employers will thus continue to be caste Hindus and will also be the persons who decide about new schools. Nor is it easy to find high-caste teachers prepared to teach low-caste pupils, or to persuade high-caste parents to allow their children to be taught by low-caste teachers. In time, no doubt, these constitutional provisions will begin to take effect, but it cannot be expected that customs so deeply ingrained in the life of the people can be removed by legislation in a short period of time.

The second group of fundamental liberties contains rights to freedom. Inevitably freedom of speech and assembly and similar rights are made subject to limitations, and the phrase commonly used is 'reasonable restrictions', a convenient phrase for starting a legal argument against any law that anybody dislikes. There are, however, detailed rules about arrest and detention, subjects on which many Congressmen feel strongly owing to frequent personal experience under British rule.

Subject to public order, morality, and health, freedom of conscience and the right freely to profess, practise, and propagate religion are guaranteed, though these rights do not prevent the States from making a law regulating or restricting any economic, financial, political, or other secular activity or from providing for social welfare and reform or the throwing open of Hindu (including Sikh, Jainu, and Buddhist) religious institutions of a public character to all classes and sections of Hindus. No religious instruction may be provided in any educational institution wholly maintained out of State funds, and no person attending any educational institution recognized by the State or receiving State funds may be required to attend religious instruction or religious worship unless he or his guardian consents.

Any section of citizens with a 'distinct language, script or culture' is given the 'right to conserve the same', and no citizen may be denied admission to any educational institution maintained by the State or receiving State aid on grounds only of religion, race, caste, or language. Even so, if the State of Orissa decides that Utkal University shall use Oriya as medium of instruction it is not very clear that a Bengali-speaking student gains much advantage from his right to be admitted.

Taken as a whole, the Bill of Rights does not solve the problem of diversity, for there are three fundamental difficulties which no legal drafting can overcome. In the first place, the distinctions of race, class, creed, and economic opportunity are far too deeply cut to allow of their abolition save by the growth of a new set of social conventions, a development which in the conditions of India will inevitably be a long process. The provisions of the Constitution will undoubtedly help towards the development, but the road will be long and the way will be hard. In the second place, the close family organization, which spreads itself into related 'sets' or groups, makes impartial administration free from nepotism (not to mention corruption) and favouritism extremely difficult to establish. It is unlikely that these deficiencies will disappear until caste endogamy disappears, for the 'sets' arise from marriage customs. In the third place, India will inevitably be divided by language unless the various groups are content to give up their vernaculars and adopt one language—Hindi or English or Sanskrit—for the whole country. In the absence of a comprehensive educational system, which would be difficult and costly to establish, even this solution would not be practicable for several generations.

EMERGENCY PROVISIONS

The protection which the Constitution gives to the States and to private persons will disappear during a grave emergency 'whereby the security of India or of any part of the territory thereof is threatened, whether by war or external aggression or internal disturbance'. The President may then issue a Proclamation which remains in force for two months unless before the end of that period it has been approved by resolutions in both Houses of Parliament. So long as the Proclamation is in operation the President may give directions to any State, the Union Parliament may legislate on any subject even though it is not in the Union list of legislative powers, and the rules governing the financial relations between the Union and the States may be suspended.

Further, if the President is satisfied that the government of a State cannot be carried on in accordance with the Constitution he may by Proclamation assume all or any of the functions of government of the State, declare that the powers of the State legislature shall be exercised by the Union Parliament, and suspend any part of the Constitution in its application to the State except any provision relating to the High Courts. This Proclamation, too, will be in operation for two months unless it is approved by resolutions in both Houses of the Union Parliament, when it will continue for six months but may be renewed by resolution for further periods of six months up to a maximum of three years.

While a Proclamation of Emergency is in operation the rights to liberty in the Bill of Rights are suspended, but laws inconsistent with those rights will disappear when the

Proclamation ceases to operate. Also, the President may by order declare that the right to move any court for the enforcement of such of the rights conferred by the Bill of Rights as may be mentioned in the order shall be suspended. It follows that the fundamental liberties may be suspended just when they are most needed. It is of course true that this happens in every country, but this is a reason for doubting the value of constitutional guarantees of liberty.

VIII

COMMONWEALTH RELATIONS

THE total population of the Commonwealth is now about 550 millions. Over one-half is in India; and India, Pakistan, and Ceylon make up 420 millions or nearly 75 per cent. If numbers alone counted, the centre of the Commonwealth would be somewhere about Nagpur. In fact, though, numbers alone do not count, and the 340 millions of India have less influence in the Commonwealth and in international relations than the 46 millions of the United Kingdom. Commonwealth relations are still primarily a matter of the relations between the United Kingdom and other members of the Commonwealth.

It should first be noted that, though Indian statesmen sometimes speak of an Asian *bloc*, there is no such thing. The three countries are very willing to act together when the question is one of discriminatory legislation in South Africa or the United States or of financial or technical assistance to economically backward territories. Their fundamental problems are economic, since all three have large peasant populations subsisting at or below a level at which a minimum standard of life can be maintained. They all desire to develop industries which will diversify their economies and provide employment for their peoples. But even economically they have divergent interests. If economic principles were allowed to take their course without official interference, both Pakistan and Ceylon, as well as Burma, would acquire large Indian populations, and these populations would become economically if not politically dominant. Though India is primarily an agricultural country, she is unable to produce enough food for her huge and rapidly increasing population. Emigrant labour from India is willing to go wherever employment can be found. Indian merchants, money-lenders, and industrialists are willing to emigrate wherever a profit can be made. What is more, they build up commercial houses which are wholly Indian. A European company in Colombo, for instance, employs a few Europeans as supervisory staff, but the clerks and shop assistants as well as the labourers are Ceylonese. On the other hand an Indian firm employs Indians almost exclusively. What is more, many Indians, both of the labouring classes and of the middle classes, leave their families in India, remit funds to them regularly, and ultimately take themselves and their savings back to India. No doubt the neighbouring countries gain economically through this influx of Indian skill and enterprise, but the advantages are indirect and therefore hidden, while the disadvantages are obvious. The Indian caste system as well as the prejudices of the local population forbids intermarriage, and the immigrants do not get absorbed into the general population. They create new racial and religious groups in countries which are already heterogeneous. They organize themselves politically into communal groups and use their power, as all such groups inevitably do, to their own advantage. If they feel that anything is to be gained by it, they invoke the assistance of the Government of India; nor is the Government backward in espousing their cause.

The problem is best illustrated by Ceylon, whose population of 7 millions includes 800,000 Indians. Most of them work on tea and rubber estates, where they are residential and are segregated into distinct communities. There are, however, many Indians working as labourers in Colombo Harbour or elsewhere or as bungalow servants. Where Indians are employed there is usually no Ceylonese labour and vice versa. A large part of the import trade of the island and much of the retail trade is in Indian hands, and the employees are mainly Indians. The Indians are organized politically in the Ceylon Indian Congress, which captured seven seats at the general election of 1947. These seven members are in opposition to the present Government and are therefore

in practice allied with the three Communist Parties. Where
there was no Indian candidate the Indian vote was usually
cast for Communist candidates. Alone of the political groups
the Indians voted against acceptance of the Soulbury scheme
in 1945. Whenever discussions arise between the Governments of India and of Ceylon, the Ceylon Indian Congress
sends representatives to make its views known to the Government of India. Inevitably the Ceylon Government and the
Ceylonese people look askance at this section of their population, which makes money in Ceylon but is sometimes more
Indian than the Government of India. It is true that some
of these characteristics also attach to the Europeans in the
island, but they are a few thousand, whereas the Indians are
several lakhs.

It is thus evident that, though the three countries have
common economic problems, they also have divergent economic interests. This divergence was well illustrated by the
consequences of the devaluation of sterling in September
1949. India and Ceylon at once devalued the rupee, but
Ceylon took the opportunity to break the link between the
Ceylon rupee and the Indian rupee. Hitherto, Ceylon law
had imposed on the Currency Commissioners an obligation
to pay Indian rupees in Bombay for Ceylon rupees. On
20 September 1949, however, legislation was passed through
both Houses by suspension of Standing Orders, to remove this
obligation. Pakistan went farther by refusing to devalue the
Pakistan rupee. In consequence of this difference between
India and Pakistan, trade and economic relations generally
were thrown into chaos, the Indian banks refusing to accept
Pakistan rupees and vice versa. The fact is, of course, that the
three countries are not primarily concerned with trade with
each other. Though India imports large quantities of food
and raw materials, especially jute, from Pakistan, and Ceylon
imports substantial quantities of food and textiles from India,
all three are more concerned with trade with the United
Kingdom.

This divergence of economic interests is supported by political and social differences. The historic Hindu-Muslim conflict has now become a conflict between India and Pakistan, for though both sides have tried to achieve a *modus vivendi*, some elements of bitterness remain. Indians opposed partition for so long that they inevitably feel some sense of grievance against those who brought it about. Pakistan is intensely and demonstratively Muslim, and Pakistanis remember that they were a 'backward community' in India even though the successors of the conquerors of India. The partition of India caused huge migrations both ways and economic problems which will take years to resolve. In spite of the efforts of statesmanship on both sides, therefore, the atmosphere is strained. Nor can Pakistanis forget that India is a most powerful neighbour, that Hyderabad State, which was under Muslim control, was forcibly annexed, and that no solution has yet been discovered for the problem of Kashmir, which had Hindu government but a Muslim majority.

Ceylon was culturally a part of India, and on those occasions at which people say nice things about each other reference is always made to 'Mother India' and 'Daughter Lanka'. From India, according to legend which probably has a foundation of truth, came the Sinhalese, and from India certainly came the Ceylon Tamils. Buddhism as well as Ceylon Hinduism are of Indian origin, and it was the Emperor Asoka who sent missionaries (according to legend his son Mahinda) to convert Ceylon. All these factors are mentioned in public speeches. Nationalism in the present century required a repudiation of western influence and therefore an emphasis upon Indian civilization. Mahatma Gandhi and Pandit Jawaharlal Nehru have by their personalities and their writings profoundly influenced the youth of Ceylon. The Buddhist revival under nationalist impulse has emphasized the contribution of Mother India. In fact, all the purely emotional factors have tended towards a linking of India and Ceylon.

Even so, the importance of these factors can easily be

exaggerated. Indeed, some prominent Indians—though not Pandit Nehru—have exaggerated them. If India and Ceylon were linked it would not be on a basis of equality: the link would involve the incorporation of Ceylon in the Indian Federation, and some Indian leaders have gone so far as to speak of this development as 'manifest destiny'. Such expressions inevitably cause Ceylon nationalism to rebound. Ceylon has a higher standard of living, a higher degree of literacy, a pleasanter mode of life, a less embittered social atmosphere, and a less crowded population. If the island were to be opened to unrestricted Indian immigration the Sinhalese and the Ceylon Tamils would soon be swamped by hard-working Indian Tamils and highly competent Indian business men. India thus appears as a friendly but potentially dangerous neighbour to whom one must be polite but a little distant. This aspect, too, must not be exaggerated, though it always is exaggerated in Indian press comment. It is not that India and Indians are unpopular, but that the Ceylonese, while admiring much that is Indian and feeling themselves racially akin to Indians, have a sensation of living under a mountain which might send down destructive avalanches.

These various factors have had the curious result of strengthening the relations of all three countries to the Commonwealth. The emotional factors which bind Canada, Australia, New Zealand, and some South Africans to the Commonwealth are, of course, absent, even in Ceylon. The island had 300 years' experience of the Portuguese and the Dutch before the British occupation, which came as the Evangelical Movement was liberalizing colonial practice. It had only a short— though unhappy—experience of Company rule before being transferred to the jurisdiction of the Colonial Office. On the whole it was a just and beneficent, though somewhat unimaginative, rule. Even so, a colonial power never endears itself to its subjects and the British technique in particular prevents the growth of loyalty and affection. The British officials, with few exceptions, were cold and correct—not unfriendly but not particularly friendly. The planters and commercial men segregated themselves into a separate 'society' which hardly knew that the indigenous population existed. The Britons whose names are revered in Ceylon are a dozen or more schoolmasters, mostly missionaries, whose reputations are preserved in the schools which they served.

In any event, a rising nationalism must attack the colonial power in order to strengthen itself. History is rewritten to re-establish the prestige of the colonial people. The Sinhalese were civilized while the ancient Britons were barbarians; Anuradhapura, the ancient capital, was larger than modern London—one politician, who subsequently obtained ministerial office, ventured to be more precise and said that before the British came Ceylon had 84 million people;[1] Lanka was the granary of the East; Sri Wickrema Raja Sinha, the last king of Kandy, was neither a Sinhalese nor a very lovable character, but he has become the centre of romance; 'the rebellion' of 1848 has been given some of the romantic colour that the Scots have given to Bonny Prince Charlie; and so on. It is true that with independence the sharp edge of controversy has been turned inwards, but it is essential to remember that few Ceylonese feel themselves kin to the British or have any particular loyalty to the British king.

In India the opposition to British rule was more intense and antagonism went deeper. Hundreds of years of Company rule left their mark in the nineteenth century. Even if India had not been burdened with a history, however, it is probable that much the same sort of atmosphere would have been created. In fact, some of the cheerful rogues who became nabobs were often better appreciated than the earnest and correct 'competition-wallahs' of the late nineteenth century. Besides, the Government of India, in its anxiety to be oriental,

---

[1] An anonymous manuscript of uncertain date gives 72 million. The latest official estimate of the population when Anuradhapura flourished is 4 million. The population just before the British occupation is unknown, but in the Maritime Provinces in 1814 it was 476,000 and in the Kandyan Provinces in 1831 it was 257,000.

kept up a standard of remote splendour repellent to the western-educated, who found themselves excluded from it. The caste system, too, has curious psychological effects. So long as everybody accepts it, the system creates a stable society in which everybody is content to remain in the status in which it has pleased God to place him: but in the transitional stage, when western education calls the whole system in question, its relics (which are still dominant in family life) may produce among the more ambitious young men in the castes deemed lower not only a sense of grievance but a truculence towards members of the higher castes. Since the British created a caste of their own—at least after European women came to India in large numbers—and often behaved as lords of creation, this truculence was very easily turned against them.

The Hindu-Muslim conflict also created a sense of frustration among the eager politicians. It was easier to 'blame the British' than to seek out and remove—if that were possible—the sources of conflict. The more firmly the Muslim League resisted the Indian National Congress, the more ready were both sides to turn on the handful of Europeans who kept the ring: and the antagonism of the Congress had some foundation in the probably correct belief that if the British 'quit India' the problem would resolve itself, not probably as Mahatma Gandhi believed by sweet reasonableness on both sides, but by police action and civil war.

It is probable, too, that Mahatma Gandhi's methods added bitterness to the political conflict. It is easier to rise in rebellion than to observe passive resistance, for rebellion is active and heroic, while passive resistance requires something of Mahatma Gandhi's remarkable powers of self-control. Soldiers on opposite sides rarely feel antagonistic towards each other, and fraternization is easy once the battle is ended; but the passive resister who is beaten by lathis, arrested by police who are themselves exasperated, and kept in gaol without trial for many months, develops a hatred which persists for many years.

The political environment was therefore far more embittered in India than in Ceylon, and there is no question of the development of a Commonwealth sentiment or sense of loyalty to the Crown. Though, for reasons mentioned later, India decided to stay in the Commonwealth, the decision had no sentimental background. On the contrary, though India has adopted a Constitution of British type, sentiment requires that there be an express repudiation of allegiance to the Crown. However great be the advantages of Commonwealth membership, it would not have been acceptable had it involved the allegiance to the Crown postulated by the Balfour Declaration and the preamble to the Statute of Westminster. India had to become a republic in order to maintain her self-respect, and most of her leaders have used that phrase in defending her action.

There is far less bitterness in Pakistan because few of the psychological factors which affected the Hindus affected the Muslims in undivided India. The antagonism is directed mainly against the Hindus, the people conquered by the Muslims who ultimately obtained dominance in undivided India. True, they would probably not have obtained that dominance but for British rule and English education, but the resistance of the Muslim League was directed against the 'Hindu Raj' and required that the British Raj behave impartially. Besides, Pakistan is intensely Muslim, and antagonism to Britain has developed among the Muslims only when British policy in the Near East seemed to be antagonistic to the Arab and Turkish peoples. Consequently, there is in Pakistan no profound antagonism to the Commonwealth but, on the other hand, no particular sentiment towards it.

The three countries have therefore retained their membership of the Commonwealth not for sentimental reasons but after weighing the material advantages and disadvantages. The disadvantages are easier to expound. In the first place, membership of the Commonwealth implies association with countries which, in various ways, exhibit some measure of colour prejudice. No Indian—or for that matter Pakistani or Ceylonese—politician wishes to sit at the same table as a representative of the Union of South Africa. The Australians insist on the one hand that Australia is capable of absorbing millions of immigrants and on the other hand that those immigrants must not have more than a certain—or in truth uncertain—quantity of pigmentation in their skins. If Australian policy insisted on the need for a population which could be assimilated into its social system there would be less objection, for Burma and Ceylon have discovered that for social reasons Indian immigrants cannot be assimilated. Instead, the policy is described as that of 'White Australia' and pigmentation is taken as the measure of acceptability. Finally, though the policy of the United Kingdom deprecates colour prejudice, most oriental British subjects who visit Britain— and nearly all of them who came in contact with 'European' families in Asia—find that socially there is a great deal of prejudice. There are houses in Asia which are not open to 'Europeans' because the householders, as undergraduates, heard insulting remarks about the colour of their skins. These are, of course, emotional factors; but such emotions are important to politicians who have to seek votes, and therefore they fall into the category of material disadvantages.

In the second place, association with the United Kingdom involves association with what is described as 'imperialism'. Its meaning is somewhat vague, like most terms of political abuse, but it arises from the fact that Britain possesses colonial territories—of which India, Pakistan, and Ceylon are thought to have formed part—which are, it is assumed, 'exploited' for the enrichment of the people of the United Kingdom. Historically the accusation cannot be denied if it is put in a somewhat different form. It is true enough that under the mercantilist system colonies were thought to enrich the metropolitan power even though it was also thought that the colonies benefited by the mercantilist restrictions. The fact that Britain changed her policy after Adam Smith showed that both assumptions were wrong does not in any way weaken the force of the argument; on the contrary, it is thought to strengthen it. What is more, it is easy enough to prove that Britain made a profit from the colonies under the free-trade system of the nineteenth century. British officials obtained salaries in the East which they could not have obtained at home; British mercantile houses, banks, and corporations (including the greatest of all, the East India Company) developed profitable businesses in colonial territory. The fact that the colonial peoples or, at least, some of them also profited is irrelevant to the argument. The new policy of the Colonial Development and Welfare Acts is too new to be recognized and in any case it never applied to India, Pakistan, and Ceylon. The theory of progressive development towards self-government was thought to be hypocrisy until its truth was demonstrated in the three countries, and in any case it is widely thought that Britain 'quit India' because the Indians made it unprofitable to stay. If it be true, as many still assume, that Britain controls Malaya, the West Indies, and much of Africa for its own profit, those who have recently acquired their freedom do not wish to be associated with it. Again, we are in the realm of emotions, but they are emotions which influence votes.

In the third place, association with the United Kingdom is thought to involve association with 'power politics'. Again the phrase lacks precision, but in present conditions it assumes that there is a conflict of power between what is called the Anglo-American *bloc* on the one hand and the Soviet Union and its satellites on the other. Even the educated people of India, Pakistan, and Ceylon had no occasion, so long as they were under British rule, to concern themselves with the complications of international politics. It is therefore unreasonable to expect that the problems of Europe will be fully understood in the three countries. Moreover, they are countries in which prestige, personal and national, is a sentiment of profound importance; nor have the 'Europeans', who spoke the same language even more emphatically, done anything to diminish its apparent importance. It is therefore easy to assume that power, prestige, and profit go together and that if India (say) is associated with Britain it will more or less clearly be involved in the British struggle for power, prestige, and profit.

These are not very substantial arguments and, though they influence a wide section of political opinion, they are not powerful enough to outweigh the obvious advantages of membership of the Commonwealth. If the Commonwealth had a foreign policy it is certain that none of the three countries would be willing to share it. Since each Commonwealth country develops and applies its own policy, however, it is very useful to have frequent consultations and, above all, to receive the confidential documents which the Commonwealth Relations Office sends out with exemplary regularity. India, Pakistan, and even Ceylon can on occasion add to the material thus available. In spite of the great ability of British diplomatic representatives, their reports from Asian countries are often coloured by the fact that they have few contacts outside government circles. A Ceylonese representative in Burma could develop a better acquaintance of Burmese political conditions than an Englishman, simply because more doors would be open to him and he would be more inclined to open doors than an Englishman who, in the Englishman's manner, kept himself very much to himself. Taking the world as a whole, however, this is not true; the inside story of events which is available in New Delhi or Karachi or Colombo is derived from London. Even a short experience is enough to convince a local statesman that he derives an immense advantage from being able to formulate policies after considering the material supplied by the Foreign Office through the Commonwealth Relations Office. What is more, if he desires further information, or even action, the Commonwealth machinery at once proves adequate. The High Commissioner is at hand to give whatever help his Government can provide.

This experience proves, too, that this is a much more dangerous world than appears from the debates of undergraduates. Those who are strong nationalists find it easy to understand—and indeed to exaggerate—the nationalism of other countries. At times, and perhaps at all times, it does not seem to have much justice or morality about it, and those who have achieved independence after a struggle find no difficulty in appreciating that a struggle may be necessary to defend it. It is, however, plain that in present conditions none of the three countries has or can provide adequate defence forces. Ceylon especially is open to attack by any country which has or acquires adequate sea and air power, and it is not because of emotional factors only that Ceylon is the most 'loyal' of the Asian members of the Commonwealth. It was in very great danger of invasion in 1942—in fact, nobody has yet understood why the Japanese did not decide to invade—and it realized how much it was dependent on the Royal Navy and the Royal Air Force.

The three countries are, in the main, primary producers who sell agricultural and mineral products and purchase manufactured goods. Only in India has any substantial degree of industrialization developed. Their products, too, are mainly tropical products which do not compete with those of Australia, New Zealand, and South Africa. On the contrary, they have a substantial import and export trade with these countries. The best customer, however, is the United Kingdom. The consumers' preference which they obtain, and even more the reduction of customs duties implied in 'Imperial preference', is of great value. Moreover, the sterling area is not merely an area in which sterling is freely convertible, though this in itself is an advantage, but also an area in which the financial experience of the City of London is especially valuable. Though the presence of European banks, insurance companies, and commercial houses in the

East is not regarded with much favour, economic chaos would result if they were ordered to withdraw. For the time being, and perhaps for a long time, financial and commercial relationships within the Commonwealth are too intimate to make it worth while to disrupt them by a political separation.

Finally, it must be remembered that the three countries are intellectually dependent on the United Kingdom. Science, technology, and professional and academic experience reach Asia through the English language and, for the most part, through the United Kingdom. The lawyers, the medical practitioners, the teachers, the universities, and the industrialists rely heavily on their contacts with Britain. They use English books and their professional organizations are affiliated to those of Britain. Assistance would no doubt be readily available even if any of the countries moved out of the Commonwealth, but the fact that they are within the Commonwealth imposes on the appropriate British organization an obligation which it rarely fails to realize. The importance of this factor is greater in Ceylon than in India or Pakistan, but even India would feel isolated if it were thrown wholly on its own intellectual resources with only such contacts as independent nations normally have with each other. The factor will, however, become much less important when Hindi becomes the professional language of India, as presumably it must when the official language is changed.

It is unlikely that the statesmen of any of the three countries have drawn up a profit and loss account to show the advantages of membership of the Commonwealth. They did realize, however, that—at least in the early stages of independence—there was no particular advantage in severing the link. Membership of the Commonwealth, as the former Prime Minister of New Zealand truly said, is independence with something added. For Asia the independence was fundamental, but there was no objection to the something added. It must, however, be emphasized that there is very little of the romantic loyalty which binds many citizens of the white

Dominions to the Crown. It would be more easily developed in Ceylon than in India, for Ceylon history is in very large measure a history of kings and princes. In India the trappings of royalty worn by the Viceroy have had too close an association with British rule. The establishment of a Constitution which was republican in form was a condition precedent to remaining in the Commonwealth. When it was found at the Conference of Prime Ministers in April 1949 that the other nations were prepared to acquiesce, India was glad of the opportunity to stay.

INDEX

MA